This book is dedicated to my children and grandchildren;
they are the branches of my own family, and their Sicilian heritage.
As they proceed with their own journey in life, my prayer is that they
awaken the love and courage within them.

This wonderful book is for you the reader, to reignite your own memories.
Place your own photos in these pages; this is my gift to you, spill wine, laugh, create your
own memories through food, enjoy the spirit of love and family this book gives you.
My desire is to spread love, and courage into your life, and extending it to others.

INTRODUCTION

> "Mangia bene, ridi spesso, ama molto."
> "Eat well, laugh often, love much."
>
> Rosaria Salmeri Amato

Cooking is the centre of my family, it represents the men and women of who we are,
I would like to introduce you to the women in my family and their recipes as you read,
you will learn more about us and the impact of our `Cucina Povera'.

Above image from left: Carmela Maiorana Amato, (Nonna Carmela). Santa Parisi Salmeri, (Nonna Santa). Rosaria Salmeri Amato, (Mamma) and me.
Left image from left: My Zio Nino (nonna Carmela's brother) zia Pasqua, (great aunt) Bisnonna (greatgrandmother) Fortunata – nonna Carmela nonno Giovacchino.

Hello,
I'm Carmela D'Amore.

I invite you to come on a culinary and personal journey with me.

I was born into a Sicilian family that migrated to Australia. I'm a chef, a mother and a storyteller. If you are searching for a book packed with themes of strength and courage, truth and freedom, history, culture and cooking - then this is the book for you.

Carmela's Cucina Povera

In this book I introduce to you my and my family's cooking style, Cucina Povera. Cucina Povera means 'poor kitchen' in Italian, and it's all about recipes for seasonal produce that's packed with flavour. I am proud to open the doors to these flavours and the stories of Cucina Povera to you.

My cooking may not attract Michelin stars, but it contains centuries' worth of life. You'll find stories of war and famine, of laughter, family, love and courage.

COOKING – A JOURNEY TOWARDS ORIGINS, MEANING AND HEALING.

I know that many children of Sicilian immigrants have faced similar struggles to me. In writing this book I was able to reach out; to acknowledge that being born into Sicilian culture has made us different. We worked hard at finding our own identity, creating our own roots, our own unique pathways – by embracing the best from our cultures, and making a life that we can be proud of.

When my parents passed away, I asked myself many big questions: What is my purpose in life? What legacy do I want to leave behind for my own children? Just hard work, or something more?

Through my writing I found many of the answers to the questions that have been burning inside me for decades. They were big questions, questions of identity. It was a search for meaning, belonging, family and culture.

I realised that whenever I cooked I learnt valuable lessons and found purpose in life. Through my cooking I discovered connection, truth, meaning and healing. I gained the strength, the courage and the patience that finally brought me to a place that enabled me to write this book and share my story. A story that is so similar to many of other immigrants yet unique. In this book I am sharing my journey and my pursuit to understand my family's origins, their roots and their stories. And, if you too are searching, I hope it will help you find and understand yours.

MY FAMILY, MY LOVE, MY RECIPES.

Each recipe that I am sharing with you in this book is filled to the brim with my nonna's and my mother's love, their patience and their history. The memories that are attached to each recipe were previously hidden in the depths of my soul.

We all have a destiny in life, and finding our equilibrium takes time, patience and the search for truth. What we all have in common is the struggle of the mind and the soul, and finding the balance between the two where peace and freedom resides. Through my own personal journey I found peace and discovered a newfound freedom.

Creating and sharing these recipes with you, I have found the place where I belong in life. Please sit back and enjoy these recipes that have been created with love, patience, kindness, and courage.

I look forward to seeing you in my kitchen.   *Carmela D'Amorè*

CONTENTS

Part 1 The Journey: Finding My Way

Part 2 Roots: Discovering Your Origins

Part 3 Fusion: Discovering the Old, Embracing the New

Part 4 Trailblazing: Celebrating the New Generation

Part 1 - The Journey: Finding My Way

14 My Story
28 Who Am I?
30 The New Kid in Town: the Three Major Challenges I Faced
32 The Seven Key Issues that Stemmed from My Three Biggest Challenges
36 Memories

Part 2 - Roots: Discovering Your Origins

44 Embrace Who You Are (Abbracia Quello Che Sei)
46 Baking the Best Bread
53 Primi Piati - Spuntini (Bite, Snack, Appetiser, Entrée)
84 Vegetable Dishes
92 Using the Best Ingredients
96 How to Make Great Pizza Dough
106 Cooking with Fresh Herbs
108 Exploring Sicilian Wines
110 Knowing Your Pasta Varieties
114 Cucina Povera Recipes for Pasta
130 Carciofi Ripieni: Fusing More Cucina Povera Recipes
134 Fun with Frittata

Part 3 - Fusion: Discovering the Old, Embracing the New

140 Acceptance
143 Salads
149 Fish
160 Examples of Fusing Cucina Povera Recipes
164 Soups
172 Veal Recipes
178 Stuffed Eggplants or Red Capsicum

Part 4 - Trailblazing: Celebrating the New Generation

182 Making My Own Trail
184 Revisiting the Three Biggest Challenges I Faced... and the Mistakes That Stemmed from Them
187 Looking after My Health
190 Self-Healing Through the Art of Cooking
191 Food Intolerances
194 Sweets
203 Espresso Coffee
206 Celebrating the Next Generation
207 Principles

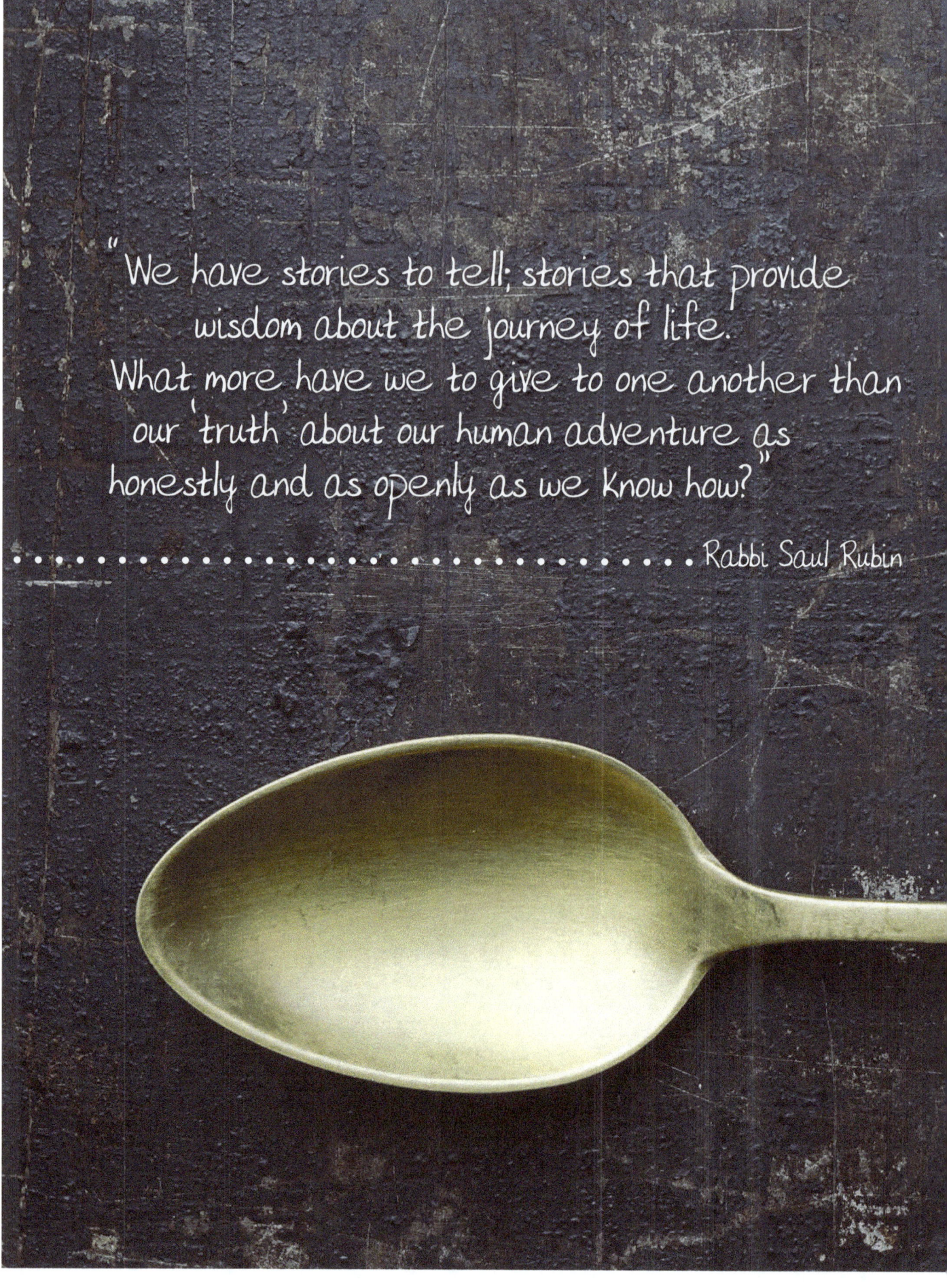

"We have stories to tell; stories that provide wisdom about the journey of life. What more have we to give to one another than our 'truth' about our human adventure as honestly and as openly as we know how?"

.... Rabbi Saul Rubin

PART ONE
THE JOURNEY:
FINDING MY WAY

MY STORY

My name is Carmela D'Amore. I am the voice of my Sicilian culture and of my family, the past, the present and the future.

I am the daughter of Sicilian immigrants. My father Salvatore Amato came to Australia in 1954 and mother Rosaria (Sarina) Salmeri arrived in 1956. This book is all about my journey of self-discovery – finding out who I am and blazing a trail of courage that has been forged over many generations.

Writing this book, I wanted to create a path for my children and their children. I wanted to show them that although life brings many challenges, the way we perceive them and draw upon our strengths to face them can go a long way towards helping us face these challenges.

I know that my experiences as the child of immigrants were not unique and that the struggles I faced growing up in Australia were the same as those faced by many others. I feel as though I am one of the lucky ones to have found peace and personal strength through my cooking – and discovering a love of my heritage.

I have rediscovered recipes from my mother's and grandmother's generations and I have created new recipes from them, which fuse the past and the present, without compromising their original value. Had I not written them down, they would have been lost forever – lost to family and friends.

Through this book I hope to ensure my children and grandchildren can see and understand, through my own eyes, their heritage. Today they are too young to understand. In time, they will be able to read the stories of my heritage and theirs.

Sometimes, life throws things at you and you are gently forced to change and let things go. Reflecting on the happy times and the struggles during my life, I found that Cucina Povera followed me and has been with me my entire life.

What is Cucina Povera?

Cucina Povera is a peasant style of cooking that originated in Italy. Its literal translation is 'poor kitchen'. The cooking techniques used in Cucina Povera are very straightforward and rely on seasonal ingredients that are in abundance.

The creative spirit of Cucina Povera

The spirit of Cucina Povera is about being creative with the ingredients available to you. It's about 'making do' with what's fresh and local. Of course that meant something very different 40 years ago when I first began my Cucina Povera cooking journey.

Cucina Povera: then and now

When Cucina Povera was created, Italians used whichever ingredients were available. In the Italian summer, when borlotti beans were in season, people would freeze them to ensure they had plenty for the year. When tomatoes were in abundance, families cooked and bottled them.

I've modified the Cucina Povera that my parents and grandparents taught me by incorporating organic ingredients. Today's much younger chefs tend to take a different approach to Cucina Povera, giving more attention to presentation and less to flavour.

These days, we are so privileged, we don't have to 'make do' with so few ingredients. Rest assured my recipes are simple, quick and easy – so in no time you will be cooking delicious, nutritious Cucina Povera, with confidence for your family and friends!

CREATING MY OWN CUCINA POVERA WITH COURAGE

My Cucina Povera: a fusion of past and present

My Cucina Povera represents the culmination of my own journey that distils Australian and Italian cultures and cooking styles. Creating my own Cucina Povera has been a life-changing journey of self-discovery. It's given me the opportunity to ensure that this style of cooking and the recipes from my mother and grandmother's generations live on for decades to come!

Where did each of the recipes in this book originate? I used to sit in the kitchen of my mother, Sarina, in Campbellfield in the 1960s, watching at arm's length, as she whipped up dishes like cannelloni with meat and Napoli, baked in the oven.

Every time I try to recreate my mother's Napoli dish, it never comes out the way my mother made it! My mother had decades of experience. It was her dish. She had created it and knew every step. Watching her cook, I could see where her own memories of her mother (my nonna, Santa) came from. It was as if her mother was in the room with us (which I'm sure she was!).

My nonna, Santa, would not allow me to ask even the simplest of questions! There was no note taking – and no recipes left for me to follow. Everything I have created in this book has been recalled from memory and recreated from those kitchen sessions with my mother and nonna Santa. Piecing together the times with my nonna was like building a gigantic jigsaw puzzle. With much courage and determination, the pieces finally came together!

I'm proud of having had the courage to preserve what's left for my grandchildren. To quote a famous (and timeless) saying from Benito Mussolini that resonates deeply with me – "meglio un giorno da leone che cento da pecora", which roughly translates to "better being a lion for one day than a sheep for 100 years."

"meglio un giorno da leone che cento da pecora"

MY GRANDFATHER'S STORY

My grandfather's story

My journey starts with Giovacchino Amato, my nonno (grandfather), or Jack, as he was also known. Jack was my teacher. I am the person I am today because of him. Nonno Jack was one of the pillars of my foundation. He gave me the wisdom and the truths to accept who I am and to be a strong individual. He taught me to embrace my culture and to build the foundations of my own journey. Observing the way that he approached life and family, my nonno taught me that actions speak louder than words.

Nonno Jack was the patriarch of his family. He weathered storms and enjoyed the rewards, through great and challenging times. Despite being illiterate, Jack managed to bring a family to a new world and give them a new life, using his eyes, his strength and his courage.

In my own journey towards becoming the matriarch of my own family, my nonno Jack was one of my pillars.

Jack's journey to Australia

Jack travelled to Australia from Falcone, Sicily, in 1956. He was already 57. He left Sicily with my grandmother Carmela in search of a better world and a better future for their children and grandchildren. Jack brought with him his own mindset from his parents and family, culture and character. He had lived a life in Sicily as an established fisherman, working with his sons Giuseppe, Nunzio, my father Salvatore, Antonino and Giovanni.

Jack left his sister, other relatives, and all that he knew and grown up with. He must have had a sense of his future in Australia, with hope for the next three generations of this family. Just the thought of leaving behind the people I love, my friends and family, all that I know gives me the shivers. Having to learn a new language, to adapt to a new way of life, a new culture, everything! Where would you start? How would you start?

MY FATHER'S STORY

When my father, Salvatore, came to Australia in the 1950s, he was just 24 and my mother was 22.

My mother had high hopes about building a future here and for the many others that she and my father helped to settle in this beautiful country. There were so many people that I can remember staying with us in our home in Kensington in Victoria.

My parents worked so hard. They worked, day and night and on weekends, to build a future, as did many others who travelled to Australia in those days.

When my father first came to Australia he worked in a Bradmill factory in Footscray and later in the 1960s, in a catering business called Maggiore Catering Business.

My mother's story

My mother worked three jobs. She worked as a tailor at night during the day mum was a seamstress for Fletcher Jones and on weekends she worked with my father in catering. Like my father, my mother had a passion for cooking. She also worked for a Jewish small business owned named Mrs Gallo who ran her own clothing business. Mum would make dresses and alterations for her during the evenings and on weekends.

My mother was one of eight children: Maria, Gaetana, Thomaso, Andrea, Rosaria, Anna, Giuseppina and Antonina. They were a very loving and tight-knit family, who always had each other's best interests at heart.

My mother once told me a story about how they could not afford to buy toys. Her mother, Santa, asked each child what they would like for her to bring home after doing the grocery shopping. Each one told her what they would like her to bring back and she smiled with her beautiful smile and amazing blue eyes, saying yes my gioies (joys), I will do my best. When she returned from shopping, she looked so sad. Looking deeply into her children's eyes, Santa told them, "Oh! I am so sorry to tell you that the old man that supplied all of the items that you wanted has passed away, so I could not bring them to you."

So she spent all of the afternoon making dolls out of old clothes and being creative with my mother and loving her children. That was all she had to give. In hindsight, looking at what mum used to say about this, it did not matter that they did not have what they wanted. My grandparents gave them an abundance of love that sustained them through the generations to come.

I suppose, thinking back, it was a white lie but it was the best that she could do without breaking their hearts. But nonna Santa and nonno Stefano left a legacy that money cannot buy. They left everyone of their children love, a generation of pure love, that I saw interweaved in every one of them. Today this is another pillar in the foundations of my life.

ABOUT ME

I was born in the Victorian town of Kilmore, in a cafe called the Bluebird Cafe. My mother said that I was born amongst food. My parents, who worked in the food industry ever since they first came to Australia, managed many restaurants – including a pizza restaurant known as The International Restaurant (in 1975 in Rye) on the Mornington Peninsula.

My paternal nonna Carmela, my father's mother, was an amazing cook. I had the pleasure of growing up with her, as she and nonno Jack lived with us. Both nonnas and my mother are the benchmarks on which I base my own Cucina Povera.

My maternal nonna (my mum's mother) Santa Parisi, whose name means saint, was also an amazing cook. Nonna Santa lived in Sicily. I got to meet her when I was 10 years old. My parents took us to Sicily on a journey to see my mother's family in Milazzo, Sicily.

My mother used to tell me that people from the town would ask Santa to make meals for them when they had guests, because of the flavours that she would weave into her meals. Santa ran cooking 'master classes' before they were invented, before World War Two in Sicily in the 1940s and the 1950s. In fact, she was the master of Cucina Povera before the term was even coined!

My mother often used to tell me that Santa was indeed a saint, with the bluest eyes. My nonno, grandfather Stefano Salmeri of Milazzo Provincia Messina Sicilia, used to tell me that he married Santa because she was beautiful.

Stefano Salmeri's story

Born in Milazzo, in the province of Messina, Sicily, my maternal grandfather Stefano Salmeri was named after the patron saint of his city, Santo Stefano. His father, Thomaso Salmeri, was a tuna fish expert. Nonno Stefano was known as Rais Stefano, meaning 'leader and chief of your territory'.

He fished for tuna as a young boy watching his father and took up his father's trade. He raised eight children during the Depression and survived two wars. He continued to fish until 1966 when tuna fishing was phased out.

The peninsula that extends from the Sicilian coastline towards the Aeolian Islands is home to the city of Milazzo. It is three cities in one, with a diverse mix of architectural styles.

Overlooking the city of Milazzo is the Norman Castle with its ancient walls that date back to 1500. The old city centre, or borgo, lies in the shadow of the castle on the foot of the hillside and contains many examples of striking medieval architecture.

The modern city is located on the coastline near the port. While modern when compared to the borgo, some of the buildings in this area date back to the 1500s. Even though Milazzo is known for fruit and flower production, the people of Milazzo are very attached to the sea.

To this day, Milazzesi continue to honour the Saint San Francesco of Paola, the patron Saint of Sailors, Saint Antonio of Padua, who took refuge on the Cape and Saint Stefano, the patron Saint of the City. Naturally, they ask for 'good fishing'.

You can read more about Stefano's story here:
http://spazioinwind.libero.it/gastroepato/tonnara_3.htm
www.youtube.com/watch?v=QImmX1EAqss cantierinavalimilazzo7.blogspot.com/

STEFANO AND SANTA: A LOVE STORY

I would like to share with you the story of my grandfather Stefano Salmeri that my mother always told me.

Stefano loved Santa from the very moment he met her. He was absolutely in love. He was six foot tall and she was just a little over four feet. The love that these two people shared passed through to my mother and to us and has enriched the generations that followed. Their love was so rich and deep that they had eight children. They passed away from heartache within 10 days of each other.. It was a different love. They held hands and kissed until they both crossed over to Heaven.

Courage and strength from Jack and Carmela

Nonno Jack and Nonna Carmela believed in working hard and saving, because to leave their family to give their children a better life in another country is a selfless love. They gave us the comfort of a family home and a model for love that has been passed down through the generations of my family. They left a land of beauty, as there was no potential for prosperity.

My parents and grandparents and many other Italian immigrant families like them, left behind a land of history, beauty and poets; a land of culture and olive trees. They left because their country offered few prospects for their families and the generations to come.

I am neither Sicilian, nor Australian

Even today, as a Sicilian born in Australia, my mother language is Sicilian dialect. I am classed neither as Sicilian nor Australian. When in Sicily, as a child and as an adult, the locals didn't understand me. I spoke a dialect with an Australian accent. My voice spans two very different worlds – with echoes of my fatherland and the love of my homeland, Australia.

Here is a poem by Di Gaetano Lino about what it means to be Sicilian. It is written in Sicilian dialect. This poem encapsulates everything that I feel as a human being about being born Sicilian.

I Am Sicilian by Gaetano Lino

"Sugnu sicilianu (siciliana)
E lu dicu cu lu me cori chinu di unuri,
Cu la peddi chi s'arrizza pi lu piaciri.
Chi avi pi figgi, gioia e tragidia, amuri e odiu;
Sta terra chi fu' pi anni matri di centu genti,
E sangu di centu genti scurri nta li me vini.
Sangu di li greci antichi e di romani,
Sangu di li nurmanni e di li paladini,
Sangu di Spagna e sangu di lu saladinu.
Sugnu sicilianu (siciliana) sugnu anticu;
Sugnu tortu e forti, comu l'arbulu d'alivu,
Sugnu spinusu e duci, comu li ficud'innia.
Odiu e vinnitta, amuri e grazia,
Sunnu la me vita,
Rispettu e unuri supra a tutta.
Sugnu sicilianu (siciliana)
Nasciutu mmenzu a li vigni di li muntagni,
Vattiatu nall'acqua salata di lu mari.
Sarbaggiu sugnu, comu lu ventu di sciroccu,
Cu lu focu di lu vurcanu dintra lu cori.
Sugnu sicilianu (siciliana) e me nni vantu
Lu dicu forti, lu dicu cu lu pettu vunciu.
Figghiu (figghia) di sta terra sugnu, do sta
Sicilia antica,
Ca fici pi matri e centu e centu genti.
Sugnu sicilianu (siciliana)"

English translation:

"I am a Sicilian,
And I say it with my heart full of honor,
With my skin all goosebumps from delight.
I am a son (daughter) of this land,
this Sicily,
Who's given birth to joys and woe, to love and hate;
This land which has been mother of a many peoples,
And the blood of many people run inside my veins.
Blood of the ancient Greeks and Romans,
Blood of the Normans and the Paladins,
Blood of the Spaniards and the Saladin.
I am Sicilian, I am old;
I am crooked and strong, like an olive tree,
I am spiny and sweet, like the prickly pear.
Hatred and vengeance, love and grace are both my life,
And most of all respect and honour.
I'm a Sicilian,
Grown up amidst the vineyards in the mountains,
Baptised with the salty water of the sea.
I am wild, like the sirocco's wind
With the volcano's fire in my heart.
I am Sicilian and I'm proud of it.
I say it loud; I say it with my swollen chest.
I am a child of this land, of this
ancient Sicily,
Who was mother of a hundred people.
I am Sicilian."

And so my journey begins and slowly unfolds like a masterpiece. The journey of discovering who I am, finding myself and my place in the world. Finding the pieces that fit into the puzzle, where bits and pieces of the past and the present belong. Unravelling the cultures in my own life and taking what was and is best and creating new beginnings for my own 'tree of life'.

"my own tree of life"

WHO AM I?

As a child in Australia in the 1960s, life was not easy. We were not well educated like we are today.

As a young child and as a teenager I attempted to live a double life, with a foot in two worlds: Australian one minute and Sicilian the next.

When I was a young student I wanted to be like any other Australian kid. At home, however, I was the Sicilian daughter of Sam and Sarina.

I simply wanted to fit in – but I didn't. I didn't like going to school. With a lunchbox packed with mortadella, salami and frittata, I was often teased and called a 'wog' or 'dago'. You were reminded of the fact that you were a wog or a dago every time you opened your lunchbox.

Faced with these social pressures, I became anti-social. My health suffered, too. I became extremely anxious. I was too afraid to eat … until I got home, of course – where I binged on food.

As the saying goes, "You cannot serve two masters and you either end up loving one and hating the other".

Decades later, as an adult and a parent of four beautiful adults, I have come to accept and embrace my Sicilian heritage and my 'Australian-ness'. It has taken decades to accept that I am part of two worlds and that I am forging my own, unique path.

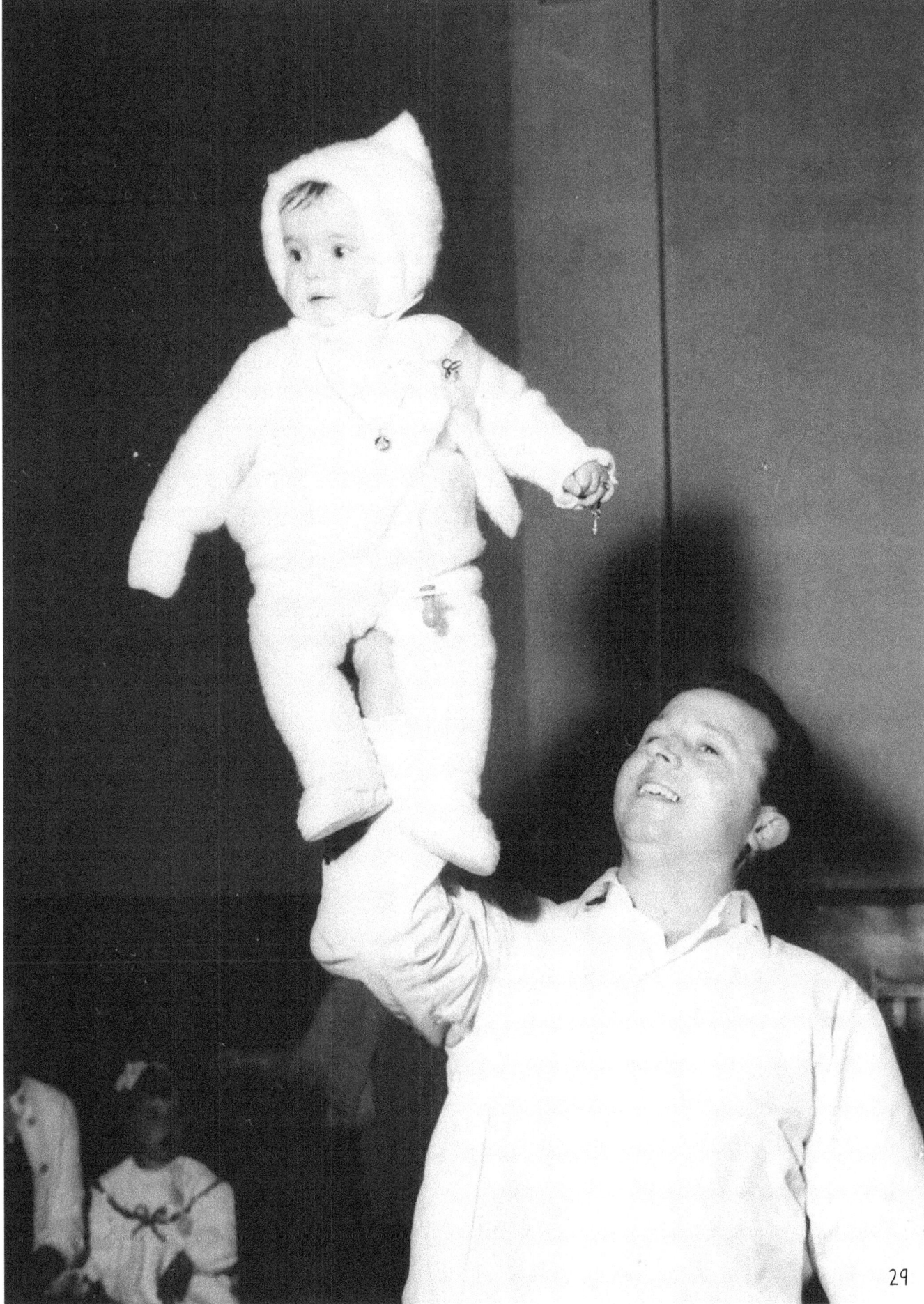

THE NEW KID IN TOWN: THE THREE MAJOR CHALLENGES I FACED

Many immigrant families that I encountered – from places like Greece and Malta, for example – encountered problems with suicide, risk-taking behaviours, drug and alcohol abuse, anxiety, depression and self-esteem issues. Growing up in Campbellfield in the 1960s I faced three major challenges:

1. Dealing with social isolation

2. Accessing education

3. Maintaining good health.

1. Dealing with social isolation

Like many children of immigrants, I found it challenging to navigate the social structure that went with the Australian way of life. To begin with, my parents were extremely strict. They used strong discipline to counterbalance what they perceived to be a very permissive Australian society. There was one set of rules for Sicilian Carmela and another for Australian Carmela, so it was a confusing time for me.

As we were very private people, we didn't discuss problems that were going on at home with anyone. At the time I was unable to speak up or speak out. To do that would have been a family betrayal.

To make matters worse, I joined a new primary school, St Brendan's, in Kensington. Attempting to make new friends, I came up against inevitable language barriers. Speaking Sicilian dialect, understanding people who spoke to me in Italian was impossible! Italian wasn't spoken in our home – only Sicilian dialect. This made maintaining any friendships very difficult.

2. Accessing education

From when I was very young, I always wanted to fulfil my dream of becoming a judge. This was not to be.

Language barriers and cultural differences interrupted my schooling and did not allow me to understand the process of the education system.

To complicate things even further, when I was 15, my family relocated me from Campbellfield Upfield High School to Rosebud Secondary School on Victoria's Mornington Peninsula. I became the only Italian among a group of surfies. I spent most of that year burying my head inside the waves, instead of my schoolbooks. Talk about becoming a 'fish out of water'!

It was impossible to communicate with my parents and tell them what was happening, as they could not understand how the changes around me were affecting me. I could not speak to people at school, either, as they did not understand my Sicilian culture. It was impossible! I had to weather this storm, on my own and find a place that I could come back to as I grew older and find healing.

3. Maintaining good health

I suffered from depression from the age of 15. Depression is something that you cannot see, yet is visible to those who can see with the eyes of the soul.

My own depression came from me being unable to be in control of my own life, because I was told what was required of me. I tried to make sense of the two worlds in which I lived, but it was impossible to find the middle ground at such a young age. I was young and wanted to travel and go to university, which became impossible. School life was totally different to my home life. So my health suffered, as I then became anorexic from stress and depression. Funnily enough, I always maintained the courage of a lion to go on.

THE SEVEN KEY ISSUES THAT STEMMED FROM MY THREE BIGGEST CHALLENGES

Torn between two worlds

I was caught between two cultures and two sets of values. With old-fashioned views on social issues like sexuality, relationships, the roles of men and women, education and employment, my parents restricted my social circle. To my parents, allowing me freedoms they had never experienced would have meant they would lose touch with their traditions and culture.

From my early teenage years I wanted to become a judge but I couldn't finish my schooling. With communication barriers, I felt dumb. Faced with so many barriers, I had many ambitions but nowhere to channel them.

From these three challenges came seven even bigger hurdles/problems:

> I was unable to communicate, or to express myself freely (with family, friends, teachers peers).

> I was unable to find direction in life.

> I was unable to embrace change (with a foot in both worlds).

> I became socially isolated – unable to have relationships with friends or family.

> I became afraid of letting go of old beliefs.

> I became negative about my life and everything around me.

> I was not gentle with myself, or kind to myself (which you need to be when you are growing up).

Looking back, it was challenging to determine how best to connect with my heritage.

"I mei radici?"

Growing up

In the years since, I have become a mother of four beautiful children who are now fully grown adults. Growing into the role of motherhood is a beautiful thing and it has been a journey that has helped me evolve into an even stronger person.

Observing the traits of generations through the birth of children

When a child is born, it has the DNA of both parents and it's easy to recognise the traits of many generations in that child. The noun, fusion, comes from the Latin word fundere that refers to combining, unification, union, the state of being combined into one body. Each child that is born has traces of the generations of each parent. You see the features and characteristics of parents and grandparents and you see yourself in each one of your children. I see courage and strength.

My strong roots helped me move forward

To connect the old with the new required 'accetare' or self-acceptance and a commitment to embracing change. It also meant needing to find inner courage, strength and determination to go forth with confidence.

Why do I call them roots? We have roots in our DNA. They are in all of us and we need to allow them to grow strong within us. Through my life journey I have merged two cultures within myself – selecting the elements that work and letting go of those that didn't.

Changing my mindset

My generation was never taught how to deal with choices. We were simply told what to do and how to do it. I found that as I grew older I had to learn to let go of the things that held me back.

I let go of old mindsets that were handed down through the generations of my grandmothers and embraced the newfound life choices that were available to me.

For instance, I needed to let go of the idea that I could keep my children at home until they married. I have recognised that my children need to spread their wings – to explore life and to travel. >>>

During my early adult life I was not allowed to do any of these things. I've changed my ways, letting go of the old ways, to do what's right for today's generation that's taking shape now.

I let go of the old ways of living, but I kept the love and the happy memories that have enriched my soul.

I found freedom in being able to choose what was right for me and for my family. In finding that freedom, I had to let go of each of my children, allowing them to pursue their own lives. In doing that they have freedom to be the person they are created to be.

I accepted that I could not grow if I held onto the past and by letting go it freed me to pursue my journey and grow.

A story about old mindsets

I would like to share an analogy with you about old mindsets.

I can make a beautiful meal, but if I have ingredients that are out-of-date or are unavailable, I have to replace them with what is available in the present day. Without being willing to make changes to my recipes, I would be unable to cook and share them with my family and friends and pass them down to future generations.

Embracing new beliefs

I believe that we have to update our belief systems and change them in line with what's happening in our lives today. We are human and we constantly evolve – our beliefs change as we grow. We cannot bring old beliefs into a new world or into a new life. We have to be able to accept that change is inevitable, that it's our deep-rooted values that shape us. We can keep them, because they are what define us as human beings.

My parents brought their old mindset with them when they came to Australia and they were never able to change with the times. They faced a constant struggle because they could not and did not, have the tools to change.

In hindsight, they probably thought that they were betraying their heritage by changing their ways of thinking and living. They would have seen change within their own families – and even more so when they returned, many times, to friends and family in Sicily. It was only through time and enduring much hardship that they were forced to see different perspectives.

Finding the tools to change our mindsets

What is best is to find the tools to help us change our mindsets. In doing that, I sought professional advice to help me replace the ingredients in my Cucina Povera recipes, without losing their 'essence'.

I have accepted that I can function in today's world without letting go of my original recipes, but that to do so I must be adaptable in my approach to cooking.

I have also accepted that if I didn't adapt, my recipes would have had to stay on the shelf, unused and uncooked.

I accept that I have freedom to experiment with what's here today – here and now.

I have learnt to let go of my fears and to embrace the changes in my life and live my life according to what is best for me and respect those around me.

I have learnt to be gentle with myself, to be honest with myself and in doing that I have become my true self, as authentic as the day that I was created, learning from my past and embracing my future, taking the good and learning from the challenges and turning my challenges into wisdom.

There is a saying that goes:

> "In the end these things matter most:
> How well did you live?
> How well did you love?
> How well did you learn to let go?"
> — Gautuma Buddha.

"Memory is the treasure house of the mind wherein the monuments thereof are kept and preserved."

Thomas Fuller

MEMORIES

Memories are like flames in my soul. Cooking allows me to ignite these flames and stay in the present and remember the past. By acknowledging the past, I can create a better world for my family and me because the past teaches me and shows me that the future is now and that this very moment is all that I have to give it my best.

Cooking allows me to unpack and dust off old memories and breathe life into them for a while. They're my memories of childhood and of my parents and grandparents.

My parents brought their Sicilian food culture to Australia and they taught me everything I know about Cucina Povera. Today there are many types of cuisine available, but one that is timeless yet can be adapted with the times without losing its uniqueness is Cucina Povera. Relying on fresh, seasonal produce, Cucina Povera is fast becoming one of the world's most recognised cuisines. It has slowly weaved its way through the centuries and is the base and foundation of Italy's kitchen that we eat in today's world.

Cucina Povera and identity

We all have a place in our memories where we remember sitting at la tavola (the table), sharing a meal with family or friends. Food touched our hearts. It made us feel warm and comfortable and loved – and we knew who we were with it. I knew who I was at that time – the food connected me and made me understand who I was. For me, food was central to the day and I couldn't wait to see what my mother had lovingly prepared for us.

Cucina Povera:
Aromas that unlock long-gone memories

Memories of my mother cooking with my grandmother are embedded into my soul. I remember sleeping in on a Sunday, smelling the aromas, following them down the hallway, greeting me and telling me gently to wake up to a Sunday lunch. The smells travelled down the hallways and out into the street. Talking about them unlocks those moments that are frozen in time. The flames that are in my soul are always there for me.

Igniting the flame within you

Back in the kitchen, knowing how high or how low to turn the flame comes with experience. The flame within me – and the one that I cook with – can be as high as my emotions and my passion. When my emotions and passions are high is often when I cook my best meals!

Having told you that, your life may be very different to mine – so always use proper cooking utensils and have a fire extinguisher handy! Never take the flame for granted – always take care in the kitchen.

My desire is to guide you to your own 'door' and show you that we all have memories that need to be unlocked so we can share them with our own children and pass them on to the next generations.

"Sometimes you will never know the value of a moment until it becomes a memory"
Dr Seuss

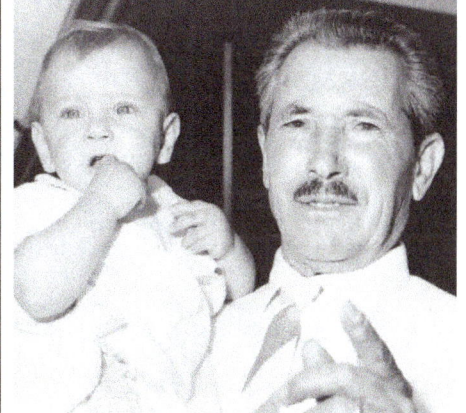

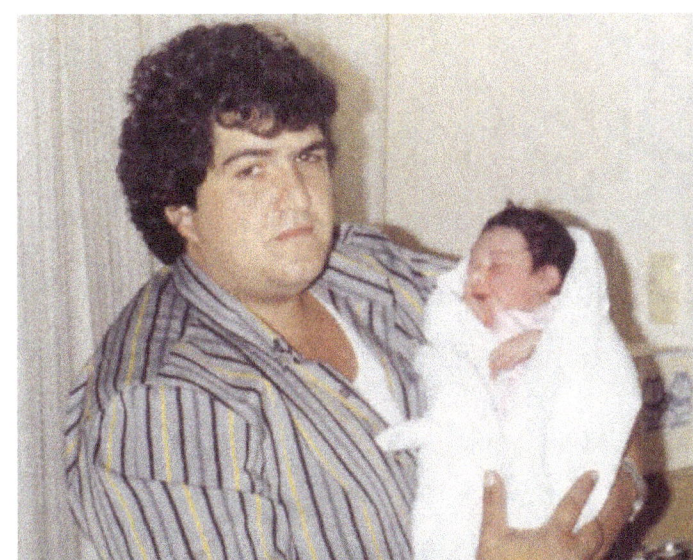

PART TWO
ROOTS: DISCOVERING YOUR ORIGINS

"People often say that this or that person has not yet found himself.
But the self is not something that one finds.
It is something that one creates."

.... Thomas Szasz

EMBRACE WHO YOU ARE (ABBRACIA QUELLO CHE SEI)

Changing my perception changed my reality, which shifted my life into a life of prosperity. Stepping out of my comfort zone gave me life. My life began at the edge of my comfort zone. One day at a time, it changed the direction in which my life was going.

La Tavola: communicating the Sicilian way

La Tavola is a tradition passed down through the generations. We sit at the table when it is time to eat. When I was growing up, we would sit at the table – La Tavola – and that was where our family's daily communication took place.

It was where everything started – wars, friendships, love stories … it was amazing growing up in a Sicilian home. I can imagine how many times our neighbour's thought we were fighting, but we weren't. We were simply communicating in our own, very passionate way.

Even today, we sit and communicate in that same, noisy, passionate way. There is never silence at our table - even though many members of my family would prefer it that way!

La Tavola: a fading tradition?

Sadly, it seems that many families sit and eat their meals in front of the television, or in separate rooms. Because of the fast-paced lives we lead, we need to remember how to communicate. I need to be reminded, just like everyone else, about the importance of communicating with family. We are so busy that we forget – and we need to be reminded that dinnertime is for eating and communicating. For most families, this is the only time that they have together. Family are the foundations of our life and I find that by having a meal, it helps you to relax and you can talk about your day. In my home we had and still have many meals where the dishes are piled up at the sink afterwards and we are still busily conversing with each other.

When a family sits down to a meal together, the spirit is one of union. An evening meal shared with family is when conversations can take place – regardless of whether you agree with each other.

I have many fond memories of childhood, sitting with my parents and my brother Joe and my grandparents at the kitchen table. It was a tradition that I continued with my own four children. It gives me comfort that I took time to continue the tradition with my own family, regardless of what was going on at the time.

"Abbracia Quello Che Sei"

ESSENTIAL SECRET INGREDIENTS

> Put on an Italian apron.
> Play Italian music - my suggestion for this one is Romantic Italia – Music (Mini – Mix). You can listen to it on YouTube, as you need a long-playing song to make good bread.
> Start with a glass of Limoncello.

BAKING THE BEST BREAD

My mum used to say that bread comes from God. Bread is a staple part of the Sicilian diet. My father had to steal it when he was a child growing up during wartime. In Falcone, his hometown in Sicily he was shot at as a child by the Germans while stealing bread because there was nothing to eat. Bread was considered more precious than gold.

In the Bible, Jesus fed the 5,000 with bread and fish. Even today bread is an important part of our meals. Bread is timeless. It has travelled through time and will continue to.

To Sicilians, bread is the core of our soul.
  Take bread away from us and we don't know how to eat.

Giuseppe D'Amore
Right of picture:

The baker: Giuseppe D'Amore

Bread played an important role in the life of my father-in-law, Giuseppe D'Amore. A baker by trade, Giuseppe used to sell bread, from the age of four, with his mother Paolina Francesca D'Amore (Cassata). Giuseppe was one of the first to open a continental bakery in Victoria – a highly successful bakery, called Conca D'Oro in Queens Parade, Clifton Hill, Victoria. It was named after the family's hometown in Palermo.

Giuseppe was a master at baking bread. I have not tasted anything as good as his. My husband Marco uses the same bread making techniques as his father. But making bread is an art that is slowly dying. Sadly, faster processes are replacing many of the techniques my family used.

Real bread takes time, as dough needs to rest. And it must be allowed to do what it does best.

CIABATTA Carmela's Cucina Povera recipe

This Sicilian bread is made with a starter dough known as 'biga'.

TIP: Prepare the starter dough the day before you plan to bake your ciabatta.

Biga, or bighino is what the starter dough is called in Italy. Used in small quantities, biga not only gives strength to what in Sicily are weak flours, it also produces a secondary fermentation from which comes the wonderful aroma, natural flavour and special porosity of the final loaves of bread.

Breads made from this starter dough develop amazing flavours because their risings are long and extract the flavour from the grain. Another benefit is that the loaves remain fresher and taste sweeter than those made with large amounts of commercial yeast.

In Sicily, bakers use dough from the previous days baking to start new dough.

I keep starter dough in the freezer as it keeps well. You can take it out and allow it to defrost at room temperature and it will become bubbly and active again. You can keep it in the fridge for about 5 days.

CIABATTA

INGREDIENTS:

- ¼ tsp active dried yeast
- 2 tbsps warm water
- 150ml olive oil
  (don't use virgin oil as it is too thick for this recipe)
- 125g high protein flour
  (Tipo 0 brand)
- 115g plain flour
  (White Wings)
- 1½ tsps salt
- 80g warm milk
- Makes 2 x 300g loaves

TIP: When I decide I want to make bread or pizza, it's usually spontaneous - I often have dried yeast packets in the pantry. You can find fresh yeast in your local supermarket in the deli section.

METHOD WOOD-FIRED OVEN/CONVENTIONAL OVEN:

To prepare the biga, combine yeast and warm water in a small bowl and set aside for 5 minutes. In a medium bowl, combine the yeast mixture with the tepid water and flour for 3 to 4 minutes, stirring until smooth.

Cover the bowl with cling wrap and leave to stand at room temperature for 12 to 24 hours.

To prepare the ciabatta, combine yeast and warm milk in a small bowl. Stir and set aside for 5 minutes. In a large bowl of a standing mixer, combine the biga, yeast mixture, tepid water, oil and flour. Mix until the dough begins to come together. Then, add salt and change the attachment to a dough hook and knead for 4 minutes.

TIP: Ciabatta dough is supposed to be sticky. Do not add more flour.

Transfer the dough to a lightly oiled bowl and cover with cling wrap. Place the dough in a warm spot to rise for 2 hours, or until the dough has doubled in volume.

Turn the risen dough onto a lightly floured board or benchtop. Using a sharp knife, cut the dough in half, shaping both pieces into a large oblong slipper shape, measuring roughly 23-25cm.

Cover with a damp paper towel and return the dough to a warm spot to rise for additional 2 hours until the dough has doubled in volume again.

Meanwhile, preheat the oven to 220°C for 1 hour.

Place a baking stone or quarry tiles on the bottom rack of the oven or wood-fired oven.

Lightly dust the pizza peel (shovel-like tool used by bakers to slide loaves of bread, pizzas, pastries, and other baked goods into and out of an oven, usually made of wood) with flour and set the first loaf on the peel. Gently shake the ciabatta from the peel onto the stone or tiles.

Bake the ciabatta for 20 minutes, removing the loaves from the oven when they are a light golden colour. Slide the pizza peel under the loaves one at a time to remove from the oven and transfer to a wire rack and cool.

BIGA

INGREDIENTS:

- 20g active dried yeast
- 2 tbsps warm water
- 5 tbsps tepid water
- 125g high protein flour (I recommend Tipo 0)

PREPARATION TIME: about 4 hours if you have the 'biga' ready

COOKING TIME: about 30 minutes.

Preheat a 220°C oven for 30 minutes. If you are using a wood-fired oven, you need to get it going at least 3 hours prior to use - make sure you have plenty of wood.

EQUIPMENT YOU WILL NEED:

Baking stone

Wooden chopping board to lay the dough on

Ceramic bowl for mixing

Cling wrap

Damp paper or tea towels

This recipe is for a conventional or wood-fired oven

· ·

Choosing the best types of flour

I like to work with high protein flours, or strong flours, like Type 00 or Type 0. These types of strengthened flours are sold as special strength flours. They may be marked as being for 'pane, pizza, dolce' (bread, pizza, baked goods).

Type 00

Type 00 flours are the softest, finest, Italian flours. They are ground to a fine powder and are very white. They are the most heavily refined, with the least fibre remaining.

Type 0

Type 0 flours are more in the range of a strong, all-purpose or lower protein bread (strong) flour. They are slightly less refined than Type 00, using about 70 per cent of the grain and are consequently a bit darker. Essentially a strong, highly refined white bread flour, Type 0 is mostly used to strengthen other flours, often mixed in at the mills.

There are also many to choose from on the supermarket shelves, White Wings is my favourite.

FRESH BREAD WITH ANCHOVIES

My mother Sarina's recipe

HOW TO CLEAN FRESH ANCHOVIES

My mother would come back from the market on a Saturday with beautiful, preserved anchovies. She placed them in a bowl with red wine vinegar and would say to me, "this is your job for this morning." It was my job to slowly wash them in vinegar until the salt was gone. Then I would pat them dry, place them on a plate and drizzle them with virgin olive oil and fresh oregano. When my brother Joe got older and was able to reach the sink, he used to help me clean them.

My brother and I would drool over those anchovies while we prepared them! When it came time to eat them, we would sit at the table with fresh bread and go for it! We were taught to eat them with the bones. The preserving process made the bones brittle and easy to digest. However when my brother was small we would peel them for him.

Slice through the bread with a bread knife and make it look like a boat. Place the anchovies, fresh oregano, olive oil, plus salt/pepper to taste and serve.

TIP: I always toast the bread. It makes it crunchier and more flavoursome when you add your favourite toppings.

There is an old Sicilian saying, "contentati con puoco e asai avrai" which translates to "be happy with little and you will have a lot". It's the little things in life that make us happy and with them we get great joy, like eating simple bread with anchovies.

"Contentati con puoco e asai avrai"

"Be happy with little and you will have a lot".

PRIMI PIATI

- Spuntini (Bite, Snack, Appetiser, Entre'e)

Spuntini in Italian means bite, snack, appetiser, entree, or tapas. In Italy, spuntini is very common, as we like to try a few different types of dishes and not stick to just one. Spuntini allows you to be more adventurous, when it comes to trying different recipes. We Italians love our food.

ESSENTIAL SECRET INGREDIENTS:

> Put on a pair of fluffy slippers
> Put on a nice Italian love song from Patrizio Buanne, like Luna Mezz'o Mare
> Kiss the one you love

CARMELA'S CUCINA POVERA

Dip for any occasion

INGREDIENTS:

> 1 x 250g tub of mascarpone cheese
> 125g anchovies or 125g tuna
> 2 tablespoons freshly diced parsley
> A squeeze of lemon juice
> Olive oil

PREPARATION TIME: about 15 minutes

EQUIPMENT YOU WILL NEED:

Food processor

Ceramic bowl

Whisk or fork

Lemon juice strainer

METHOD KITCHEN BENCH:

Place the anchovies in a bowl, mash with a fork and slowly allow the meat to dissolve. Then add the mascarpone cheese, parsley, lemon juice, olive oil and mix. Add chilli if you like your food spicy. This dip goes well with a salami board and olives.

SICILIAN PANZARELLA

MY MOTHER SARINA AND NONNA SANTA'S RECIPE

This is a meal that my mother, Rosaria 'Sarina' (Salmeri) Amato used to make for me and my brother Joe.

I have eaten it throughout my adult years. Each time I eat it I see my mother and her face, always bright and shining. She was an amazing woman. She had the rosiest cheeks. She made you feel loved just by smiling at you. I can't tell you how blessed I have been to have had a mother like her. Her face was like the sun. My mother may have passed away in 2014, but she is with me in spirit whenever I recreate this dish.

My brother Joe and I used to sit on the back porch in the sun on a sunny day and be so excited because the ingredients are simply bursting with flavours. The tomatoes from our garden, my nonno's cucumbers and onions... these flavours are rich with memories.

My nonno Jack was the caretaker of a typical Sicilian/Italian garden and 'guai'* if you touched his merchandise you could be slaughtered! It was like touching gold. We had to ask permission first.

*guai means watch out or trouble.

• •

INGREDIENTS:

One fresh loaf of treccia or split Vienna. It needs to be pasta dura bread. You might be able to get away with using ciabatta.

> 2 fresh tomatoes (diced)
> ½ cucumber (diced)
> ½ red onion (diced)
> A pinch of fresh oregano
> Virgin olive oil
> Salt/pepper to taste

PREPARATION TIME: 15 minutes

EQUIPMENT YOU WILL NEED:

Paring knife

Chopping board

Chopping knife

METHOD KITCHEN BENCH:

Carve out the inside of the bread and keep the remainder as you will need to later place it on top, like a hat to soak up the juices. Place all the ingredients into the hollow of the bread, pour in the olive oil and mix it all with your hands.

Let the bread soak up all the juices, then place the bread previously removed, on top like a hat. Let it sit.

Then you can use a small paring knife to cut strips and eat it. Or, just tear it with your hands, like a Sicilian!

It was like touching gold.
We had to ask permission first.

"A salami board keeps everyone happy and it always makes people feel welcome in my home."

PREPARING A SALAMI BOARD

NOTE: I make salami in the wintertime and they last all year. I make the pancetta and capocollo with my Calabrese friend Lina who is a gun.

PREPARATION TIME: about 15 minutes

EQUIPMENT YOU WILL NEED:

Wooden board

Medium Chopping board

Medium Chopping knife

Serving plate

When you prepare a salami board, you can use just a few ingredients. It's a typical Sicilian/Italian custom when you have visitors over for a couple of drinks. A salami board keeps everyone happy and it always makes people feel welcome in my home.

Place a few ingredients such as salami, cheese and fresh fruit on a board. Keep topping them up.

My friends love a salami board. I get to spend more time talking to them than preparing a meal. A salami board is great for any occasion.

....

CHOOSING YOUR CHEESES

Romano, Pecorino - there are so many to choose from, but I love cheese with some bite.

Extra items that you can add to your salami board

- Olives
- Semi-dried tomatoes
- Marinated artichokes
- Bocconcini cheese
- Buffalo cheese
- Fresh anchovies
- Fresh smoked Salmon

Add the anchovy mascarpone dip

Fresh vegetables like cucumbers, tomatoes and celery.

ARANCINI WITH PEAS AND PUMPKIN

Carmela's Cucina Povera and son Joseph's recipe

INGREDIENTS:

- 1x 500g packet of Arborio rice
- Vegeta stock
- 4 eggs (beaten)
- 1 cup grated Parmesan cheese
- 2 cups diced Mozzarella cheese
- ½ cup diced parsley
- 1 cup egg wash mix with milk
- Breadcrumbs for coating
- 2 cups peas (cooked)
- 2 cups pumpkin (diced)
- 1 red onion (diced)
- Flour for dipping the arancini, about 3 cups
- Salt/pepper to taste
- Oil for frying

(I always use olive oil or canola oil). It depends on the texture you wish to create. I prefer olive oil as it is fuller of flavour and you can taste the richness of the flavour.

PREPARATION TIME: about 30 minutes

COOKING TIME: about 30 minutes

EQUIPMENT YOU WILL NEED

Deep frying pan

Oven tray

Medium Chopping board

Medium Chopping knife

Cooking Pot for rice

Wooden spoon

METHOD OVEN/BENCHTOP/STOVETOP

The secret to making a delicious arancini is the way you prepare the ingredients. I usually cook the peas, pumpkin and red onions together in the oven. It takes about 15 minutes on a high heat and gives the arancini a better texture and flavour. Let the vegetables cool down before you add them to the cool rice.

Cook the rice until it is soft, which should take 15 - 20 minutes. Drain and place onto a flat tray (you can use one of the oven trays), allowing it to cool. Allow about 15 minutes. Add all of the other ingredients to the rice and mix with your hands until it feels mushy.

Then, start making balls with the palm of your hand. Make sure that they are very firm, otherwise they tend to break apart.

Dip them into the flour and then the egg wash and breadcrumb mix. Place on another tray and keep making the mini arancini.

Heat the oil in a large pan. You can test it by dropping a few breadcrumbs into the oil. When they start to sizzle, you know the oil is ready. >>>>

Place into the oil very carefully. When they are golden brown you know they are ready. If you are deep-frying them they usually takes about 4 to 5 minutes to cook. If you are shallow-frying them it takes a lot longer as you will have to carefully turn them.

Arancini are handy for those unexpected visitors. You can half-cook them and when they are cool place them into containers and freeze them. To defrost, place them in the microwave for a few minutes and then fry them. They retain their flavours and are great spuntini (bites) with family or friends.

Typical Sicilian arancini are made in the same way, but I use Bolognese sauce as the filling, combined with peas, grated egg and chunks of Mozzarella cheese. These aren't your average spuntini. They are more like a meal!

Each time I cook the arancini, my nonnas and bisnonnas (great-grandmothers) pop up to say hello to me. The flavours in the arancini are timeless.

PLAIN ARANCINI

My mother Sarina's and nonna Santa's recipe, updated by Carmela

INGREDIENTS

- 500g packet Arborio rice
- 500g grated Mozzarella cheese
- 6 eggs
- ½ cup Vegeta stock
- 3 cups Parmesan cheese

PREPARATION TIME: about 30 minutes

COOKING TIME: about 15 minutes

EQUIPMENT YOU WILL NEED

Deep frying pan

Ceramic bowl

Saucepan

Oven tray

METHOD STOVETOP

Boil a saucepan of water, add Vegeta stock and rice and cook for about 20 minutes. Strain the rice and place onto an oven tray. (I use oven trays as they are versatile and they allow you to mix ingredients well.)

Place the eggs, Mozzarella cheese and Parmesan cheese into a mixing bowl and combine using your hands with the rice until it is moist and the ingredients are sticky.

Make small balls in the palm of your hands and dip them into the egg wash. Then roll them in breadcrumbs and place them on a tray. Next, heat the oil in a frying pan and fry the arancini until they are golden brown. This should take 3 to 4 minutes depending on the heat of the oil. Place them on a large oval plate and serve, as spuntini.

PARMA CON FIGGI

Parma ham with figs

SERVES 2-3

INGREDIENTS

> 8 slices Parma ham or Prosciutto

> 5 fresh figs (sliced)

> 1 tablespoon balsamic vinegar

PREPARATION TIME: about 15 minutes

EQUIPMENT YOU WILL NEED

Paring knife

METHOD – KITCHEN BENCH

Arrange the slices of Parma ham and the cut figs on a serving dish. Sprinkle with balsamic vinegar.

TIP: Parma ham is an Italian version of prosciutto crudo, which is uncooked ham, or you can have prosciutto cotto, which is cooked ham that has been preserved and cured.

ESSENTIAL SECRET INGREDIENTS

Have your children help you make this. If you don't have children ask your nephews or nieces. Enjoy making it with them.

Have a glass of San Pellegrino Chinnotto (Italian coke) and add a slice of orange.

I used to make plain arancini for my children as an after-school snack. When they arrived home from school I would have already made them so they were ready to eat. I would have made them fresh as the cheese would just melt through. When you took a bite the Mozzarella oozed out of the arancini.

POLPETTE DI CAVOLIFIORI

(Cauliflower fritters) My mother Sarina's recipe

INGREDIENTS

- 400g cauliflower
- 1 egg
- 2 anchovy fillets
- 70g grated Pecorino cheese
- 1 tablespoon pine kernels
- 1 tablespoon raisins
- 30g breadcrumbs
- Olive oil for frying
- Sea salt and cracked pepper to taste
- ½ cup fresh parsley, chopped

SERVES 4

PREPARATION TIME: about 20 minutes

COOKING TIME: about 20 minutes

EQUIPMENT YOU WILL NEED:

Medium saucepan

Strainer

Ceramic bowl

Large tablespoon

Large frying pan

METHOD STOVETOP

Cook the cauliflower in a saucepan of slightly salted water until soft. Drain well. After draining the cauliflower you could leave the saucepan on a very low flame to remove any excess liquid.

Next, place the cauliflower into a mixing bowl and mash it with a fork. Add the remaining ingredients and mix well until the mixture is firm and shape the mixture into flat balls (about the size of a large tablespoon). Heat a little olive oil in a frying pan and when hot, fry the polpetti until the pieces are golden brown on both sides. Place them on kitchen paper to remove the excess oil and sprinkle a little Pecorino on them before you serve.

They're great as a spuntini.

polpette di cavolifiori

They're great as a spuntini.

PANELLE ALLA PALERMITANA

(Chickpea fritters) My husband Marco's recipe

SERVES 2

INGREDIENTS:

- 200g chickpea flour
- 1/2 litre cold water
- Fresh parsley, chopped
- Sea salt
- Olive oil
- Fresh lemons
- Crusty bread rolls

PREPARATION TIME: about 30 minutes

COOKING TIME: about 15 minutes

EQUIPMENT YOU WILL NEED:

Baking tray

Ceramic bowl

Wooden spoon

Medium Wooden chopping board for mixture

Aldi Frying pan

METHOD STOVETOP

Mix the chickpea flour with the water, making sure there are no lumps. Add a pinch of salt or two and a small amount of finely chopped parsley. Mix well and heat on a low flame until the mixture turns into a thick, almost solid mass. Then, place the mixture onto a baking tray and leave to cool. The thickness should be about 3 to 4 mm. Once the mixture has totally cooled and turned to a soft solid state, cut into rectangles about 7cm x 4cm.

Heat a decent amount of extra virgin olive oil in a frying pan. Add a little salt and then fry the rectangles until they are golden brown. Place them onto a kitchen roll to soak up any excess oil. Take a crusty bread roll, add a fritter or two, squeeze over some fresh lemon juice and eat while it is still hot. This is street food in Palermo, Sicily and is found all over in the marketplace. It is a very common dish to eat with friends and family.

GAMBIERI CON ROSMARINO

(PRAWNS WITH ROSEMARY) Carmela's Cucina Povera recipe

INGREDIENTS

- 6 king prawns, butterflied (you slit the back of the prawn with a paring knife and gently open it up)
- Crushed garlic
- ½ teaspoon butter
- ½ teaspoon olive oil
- ½ red chilli (diced)
- Rosemary leaves/lemon thyme leaves

SERVES 1

PREPARATION TIME: about 20 minutes

COOKING TIME: about 15 minutes

EQUIPMENT YOU WILL NEED

Medium chopping board

Paring knife

Large frying pan

Skewers

METHOD STOVETOP/GRILL

This dish needs to be cooked on a high heat. Place the oil, butter and chilli into a pan and allow to sizzle. Next, add the prawns, garlic and rosemary, letting the prawns cook for about 4 to 5 minutes. They don't need long. Most people overcook seafood and it loses its flavours and texture and becomes too dry.

Serve the prawns on a plate and you have a great starter/spuntini. To make the dish look a bit more polished, you can skewer the prawns, and cook them on the grill. Then prepare the other ingredients and drizzle onto the cooked prawns. This way you can still have the flavour without the added calories.

ESSENTIAL SECRET INGREDIENTS

- Be with someone you love
- Wear an Italian apron
- You must smell all of the ingredients
- You must hug someone and smile a lot

SALSICI DI SARINA (SICILIAN SAUSAGES)

My mother Sarina's recipe

MAKES 8-10

INGREDIENTS

- 1kg fresh coarse pork mince
- 1 tablespoon fennel seeds
- Salt/pepper to taste

PREPARATION TIME: about 30 minutes

COOKING TIME: about 15 minutes

EQUIPMENT YOU WILL NEED

Funnel

Or sausage machine

Frying pan/grill/barbeque

Oven tray or ceramic bowl

Sausage funnel

Kitchen string

You will need to get fresh intestines from any Italian butcher and wash them. I usually soak them in bicarbonate soda and wash them very thoroughly. The intestines are for you to put the pork into. They are the skin of the sausages.

Method kitchen bench/stove

Place all the ingredients in a bowl and mix.

TIP: Make sure you take an extra moment to fry up a spoonful of the sausage mix in a pan to be sure you like the flavour. Add more seasonings if required.

PREPARE THE FUNNEL*.

Next, hold one open end of a skin over your kitchen sink and turn on the cold water. Allow the water to run through the skin. This will make it easy to slip over the end of the funnel. Place the open end of the skin over the nozzle part of the funnel and push most of the skins up onto the nozzle, but leave about a two-inch tail at the end and knot it.

Start taking small amounts of the sausage and push it with your thumb into the mouth of the funnel and into the skin. Do not overfill it or it may break. Fill the skin evenly but leave about 2 inches of the skin remaining at the top unfilled. Slip the skin off the funnel and knot the end. Use a toothpick to poke little holes here and there along the sausage. This will prevent the sausage from exploding when cooking. Continue making the sausages. I like to leave it in long lengths but if you want to make links, just twist the skin every 3 or 4 inches as you fill it. Coil the sausage and place it in freezer bags. Better yet, cryovac them and freeze for up to 6 months.

*The funnel is a utensil that you can buy from your local hospitality store. It is used to make sausages. This is a great way to make sausages and the family can help you. With a funnel you don't have to use a machine. You can even make chicken mince sausages adding chives and garlic. There are many ways of making sausages but this way you know what you have put into them, and there are no preservatives.

salsici di sarina

COZZI ALLA SICILIANA

Recipe on following page:

COZZI ALLA SICILIANA

Carmela's Cucina Povera recipe

SERVES 2

INGREDIENTS:

- 2kg large fresh mussels
- 2 cloves fresh garlic (crushed)
- Virgin olive oil
- ½ cup cooked Napoli sauce (see page 127)
- ½ cup fresh parsley (diced)
- 2 sage leaves
- ½ cup black olives (halved)
- ½ chilli (diced)

PREPARATION TIME: about 20 minutes

COOKING TIME: about 15 minutes

EQUIPMENT YOU WILL NEED:

Steel scourer

Paring knife

Casserole pot with lid

METHOD STOVETOP

Clean the mussels by scraping the shells with a steel scourer and pulling the beards off. Place the mussels in a heavy casserole dish or pan with a lid with all the other ingredients and allow them to cook, to infuse all the flavours while they are cooking. They will sweat and release their water. They usually take 7 to 10 minutes to open.

When opened, you can place them into a bowl and serve with fresh bread. You can also dip the bread into the sauce. It's divine! I usually add a little pasta and have pasta and mussels. You need a lot of parsley, as it adds a nice flavour.

SALSICI FRITTI - FRIED SAUSAGES

SERVES 2

INGREDIENTS

> 4 sausages

TIP: I always pre-boil the sausages and cook them about half way. I then fry them until they're cooked through. I find this is better for me, as it reduces the cooking time.

METHOD STOVETOP/GRILL/BBQ

Cook the sausages in a pan or under a grill. Place onto a board and slice them into circles. Place toothpicks through them and you can have them as spuntini. Or make them as a meal with your favourite side dish or salad.

In Sicily, we cook the sausages on the barbeque as they have more flavour. Before we cook them we add lemon leaves that enhances the flavour and raises the taste to another level.

Sicilians love barbeques and most of our meats and fish are cooked on a raging fire. Today we have gas barbeques, but nothing beats the flavour that a real wood fire gives you.

SALSICI SICILIANI STUFATI

(Stewed Sicilian sausages) My mother Sarina's recipe, updated by Carmela

SERVES 3-4

INGREDIENTS

> 8 Italian sausages with fennel
> 1 small brown onion (diced thinly)
> 1 cup baby peas
> 2 cups diced tomatoes
> Virgin olive oil
> 1 garlic clove (crushed)
> 2 potatoes (peeled and quartered)
> 2 sage leaves
> 2 cups stock or water

PREPARATION TIME: about 30 minutes

COOKING TIME: about 90 minutes

Preheat a 180°C oven for 30 minutes

EQUIPMENT YOU WILL NEED

Casserole dish

Medium chopping board

Medium chopping knife

Paring knife

METHOD STOVETOP

Brown the sausages and onions in a casserole dish with oil. When they are half cooked, add the tomatoes and 2 cups of stock or water. Bring the mixture to the boil then reduce to a simmer, adding potatoes, peas, garlic and sage. Cook on low for about 1 1/2 hours, stirring occasionally and adding additional water or stock if the dish starts to dry out. This dish needs to be served moist (umido).

POLPETTI (MEATBALLS)

My mother Sarina, nonna Santa, and nonna Carmela's recipe, updated by Carmela

SERVES 4

INGREDIENTS

- 1kg beef mince
- 1kg pork mince
- 2 cups breadcrumbs (refer to tip)
- 2 cups Parmesan cheese
- 1 red onion (grated). Red onion is sweet and adds more flavour.
- 1 clove of garlic (crushed)
- 1 cup diced fresh parsley
- Sprinkle of rosemary leaves
- Sprinkle of lemon thyme leaves
- 6 eggs (beaten)
- Napoli sauce optional
- Salt/pepper to taste

PREPARATION TIME: about 30 minutes

COOKING TIME: about 30 minutes

EQUIPMENT YOU WILL NEED

Ceramic bowl

Frying pan

Casserole dish

Medium chopping board

Medium chopping knife

METHOD STOVETOP

Place all the meat into a big mixing bowl with the Parmesan, breadcrumbs, salt/pepper, herbs and grated onion. Make a hole in the middle of the mixture and add the eggs and slowly combine the mixture with your fingers until the texture is smooth and moist.

TIP: I always use stale bread for this as it makes the texture softer. You can soak the bread in milk for about half an hour prior to making the meatballs. I always use gluten-free bread for myself. I like the Woolworths Select brand of bread.

Then start making your meatballs. If you find that the mixture is not moist enough, wet your hands. You can also make a Napoli sauce (see page 127) and place the meatballs into the sauce and allow them to cook for about 30 minutes. Or if you just want to fry them, add olive oil to the frying pan and place the meatballs gently in the heated pan turning them over every five minutes, watching them constantly so that they don't burn.

TIP: You can pre-cook and freeze the meatballs so when you have unexpected guests, you can reheat them in the microwave or the oven.

ESSENTIAL SECRET INGREDIENTS

> A pair of dancing shoes
> Drink a glass of wine
> Listen to Italian music
> Wear an Italian apron

polpetti

CAPONATA D'ESTATE

(SUMMER CAPONATA) Carmela's Cucina Povera recipe

SERVES 2

Caponata, in Sicilian, is a dish of fried vegetables that is usually served as a spuntini. It is made up of summer vegetables such as eggplants, red capsicum and celery.

INGREDIENTS

- 1 large eggplant
- Sea salt/pepper
- 100 whole black olives in brine
- Olive oil for frying
- 1 onion (diced)
- 2 celery stalks (diced)
- 1 tablespoon caster sugar
- 5 tablespoons good quality red wine vinegar
- Vegetable oil for deep frying
- 1 red capsicum (diced)
- A bunch of fresh basil
- Virgin olive oil
- Tomato passata buy already made

PREPARATION TIME: about 30 minutes
COOKING TIME: about 30 minutes

EQUIPMENT YOU WILL NEED

Frying pan
Ceramic bowl
Chopping board
Medium chopping knife

METHOD STOVETOP

Dice the eggplant into small cubes (around 2cm). Sprinkle the eggplant cubes with salt and leave them to drain in a colander for at least 1 hour. Squeeze the eggplant lightly to get rid of the excess liquid.

Remove the pips from the olives and crush them. Heat a little olive oil in a pan, adding the onion, celery and olives and cook them until they are soft but not coloured.

Next, add the tomato passata. Mix the sugar and vinegar in a cup and add the liquid to the pan, bringing it to the boil. Then, remove the pan from the heat and transfer the contents of the pan into a big bowl.

Deep-fry the eggplants and capsicum separately. Place them onto a tray with greaseproof paper, allowing them to cool. Then add the vegetables to the mixture and Glad Wrap the bowl, allowing it to stand at room temperature for about 2 hours. This helps the flavours to infuse.

This dish is served at room temperature and usually keeps on the benchtop for a few days.

My father-in-law, Giuseppe, used to eat this dish for days in the summer, as it's a dish that keeps and is very nutritious and filling.

Sicilians love to eat food that has flavour. This dish, which contains sugar, helps to keep your energy levels up, especially when it is a hot day.

ESSENTIAL SECRET INGREDIENTS

Wear a lovely Italian dress or summer dress or shirt. Listen to Dean Martin's, That's Amore and cook with love and a smile.

CAPONATINA DI MELANZANE (EGGPLANT CARBONATINA)

Carmela's Cucina Povera recipe

SERVES 2

This is one of Sicily's most popular and most versatile eggplant dishes. You can eat it with bread as part of an antipasto or as a side dish with hot or cold meats, or fish. A caponatina is a small caponata.

INGREDIENTS

- 1kg eggplants cut into cubes the size of walnuts
- 1 large brown onion (diced)
- 2 celery hearts - inner heads only (diced)
- 150g pitted green olives
- 80g salted baby capers (rinsed)
- 500g ripe tomatoes (chopped)
- ½ teaspoon ground cinnamon
- ½ teaspoon ground cloves
- 60g caster sugar
- 60ml white wine vinegar
- Extra virgin olive oil for frying
- Virgin olive oil for dressing
- Freshly torn basil
- Salt/pepper to taste

TIP: When you select eggplants for cooking, the best ones are those without too many seeds, the only way you can tell is by buying them in season, I find that when they are out of season, they had a lot of seeds.

PREPARATION TIME: about 30 to 60 minutes

Cooking time: about 20 minutes

EQUIPMENT YOU WILL NEED

Sauté pan

Medium chopping board

Medium chopping knife

Paring knife

A clean tea towel for patting dry

Strainer

METHOD STOVETOP

Immerse the eggplant cubes in salted water for an hour, then drain them. Squeezing the water out, pat dry the eggplants. In a sauté pan, heat about 8 teaspoons of extra virgin olive oil and fry the eggplants until they are golden. I usually deep-fry them, which is easier. Scoop out the flesh of the eggplant with a slotted spoon and set aside on a plate with kitchen paper, so it can soak up the excess oil.

Adding more oil to the pan if necessary, fry the onion until soft. Next, fry the rest of the ingredients, except for the sugar and vinegar, and simmer for about 20 minutes. Mix the sugar with the wine vinegar and add to the fried ingredients with the eggplants. Taste for salt and cook for another 10 to 15 minutes.

Place the caponata in the ceramic bowl, adding freshly torn basil and serve. It can be eaten warm but is also delicious cold. It is best kept in a ceramic bowl.

POLPETTI DI MELANZANE TORNADO STYLE (EGGPLANT MEATBALLS)

My mother Sarina and my nonna Carmela's recipe, updated by Carmela's Cucina Povera

SERVES 4 FOR SPUNTINI

INGREDIENTS

- 4 medium sized eggplants cut into quarters
- 4 eggs (whipped)
- 1 cup diced parsley and 4 leaves fresh basil (thinly sliced)
- 1 cup breadcrumbs (I like the Panko brand – see the Index for bread substitutes)
- 2 cups Pecorino (grated)
- 1 garlic clove (small, diced)
- ½ cup olive oil/canola oil for frying
- Milk or egg wash for dipping
- Extra breadcrumbs for coating
- Salt/pepper to taste

PREPARATION TIME: about 30 minutes

COOKING TIME: about 20 minutes

EQUIPMENT YOU WILL NEED

Frying pan - Strainer - Chopping board - Chopping knife

Paring knife - Ceramic bowl - Saucepan for boiling

METHOD STOVETOP

Boil the eggplants in a saucepan with plenty of water, adding a pinch of salt and stir slowly. They tend to float to the top so you need to keep pushing them down, until they have soaked up the water and are half-cooked. This will take about half an hour.

Strain the eggplants and remove all the water. It's best to cook the eggplants the day before, to allow all the water to drain. But if you are in a hurry, just squeeze the excess water out of them.

Place the eggplants in a big bowl, adding all of the other ingredients. Mix with your hands (making sure they are clean). The ingredients need to be moist so that when you make the polpetti they are soft.

Place the ingredients into the palm of your hand and make a shape like a tornado. Make them small – about the size of 6cm by 3cm wide – this makes it easier to fry them and reduces the amount of oil needed.

Dip them in milk or egg wash, depending on what you prefer and then in breadcrumbs. Place them on a flat tray.

Meanwhile heat the frying pan, adding oil when you feel the heat of the pan coming up through to your palm. Or, you can place one of the polpetti in the oil, or even add some breadcrumbs. You'll know the oil is ready if the polpetti starts to sizzle. >>>

Place the polpetti in the frying pan and slowly cook them. You can see that they are ready when the breadcrumbs start to turn a nice brown. This takes about 3 to 4 minutes depending on how large the polpetti are, then turn them over and cook them for another 3 to 4 minutes. Place them on a plate. You can use greaseproof paper or a paper towel to soak up the oil.

Allow them to cool for about 5 minutes. You can also make a little side dish to dip the polpetti in.

SALSA VERDI (GREEN SAUCE)

Carmela's Cucina Povera recipe

INGREDIENTS

- ½ cup fresh parsley
- ½ cup fresh basil
- ½ cup fresh mint
- 4 anchovies
- 2 tablespoons baby capers (drained)
- Juice of 1 lemon
- ½ cup virgin olive oil
- Salt/pepper to taste

PREPARATION TIME: about 20 minutes

EQUIPMENT YOU WILL NEED

Food processor

Ceramic bowl

METHOD STOVETOP

Place all ingredients into a food processor and blend well. When you have made the Salsa Verdi, let it sit for about half an hour to allow the flavours to fuse. Now you have your Salsa Verdi ready to dip!

It's really flavoursome and you can store it in your fridge in an airtight container and it will keep for weeks.

Serve Salsa Verdi with meats, fried fish, or carpaccio.

**This next dish is one of my favourites. I use it as a side dish, next to Veal Cotoletta. You can even put it on top of a Veal Cotoletta. By adding an iceberg lettuce and you have a nutritious meal.

I will give you my recipe on how I crumb the Veal Cotoletta. For the iceberg lettuce salad I usually just break the lettuce with my hands after I have washed it, adding a little virgin olive oil, juice of ½ lemon, salt/pepper to taste and mix it all together.

CARMELA'S CUCINA POVERA COTOLETTA MIX (SCHNITZEL MIX)

My mother Sarina, nonna Santa, and nonna Carmela's recipe, updated by Carmela

Makes about 4 cotolettas/schnitzels (chicken/pork/veal)

INGREDIENTS

- Chicken/pork/veal cotolettas/schnitzels
- 3 cups Panko breadcrumbs
- 1 cup Parmesan cheese
- ½ cup chopped parsley
- 1 clove garlic, chopped (if required)
- 1 red onion, grated (if required)
- Salt/pepper to taste

PREPARATION TIME: about 15 minutes

EQUIPMENT YOU WILL NEED

Ceramic bowl

Medium Chopping board

Medium Chopping knife

METHOD BENCH

Depending on what type of meat you are cooking, you may wish to add garlic. When I am making chicken cotoletta, I add 1 clove of chopped garlic into this mix. If I am making Beef Cotoletta, I add a grated red onion to the mix. When I make a Veal Cotoletta, I don't put anything extra, as veal is tender and you need the flavours to come through.

ESSENTIAL SECRET INGREDIENTS

You require your children's help with this one or nephews and nieces

Hug them while making this and tell them you love them.

My Nonna Carmela Amato's influence on Cucina Povera

My nonna Carmela Amato (Maiorana) was another person who influenced my Cucina Povera. She made the best meals when I was a child. She raised five sons and was an amazing woman. She was known in her home town Falcone, Sicily as `Donna Carmela'.

She was born in Sicily and at the age of five, with my great uncle Nino and my great-grandfather Giuseppe and my great-grandmother Fortunata, went to America where she worked. In America they had two children, my great uncle Samuel and my great auntie Nancy. They later returned to Sicily when my nonna was 16. I was named after her. In those days many of the children were named after their grandparents, as it kept the family name alive.

When I make this next recipe and every other one that I make that are nonna Carmela's, it's like I am travelling back through time. The taste of this dish makes me think of her, her touch and her laugh. I remember the exact thing she was doing at that moment.

Our elders are our teachers. They teach us, without realising that they are doing it. I am a willing pupil.

MELANZANA BOILITA

Nonna Carmela's recipe

SERVES 2

INGREDIENTS

- 2 diced eggplants
- 1 garlic clove (crushed)
- ½ cup chopped mint
- Drizzle of virgin olive oil and a drizzle of red wine vinegar
- Salt/pepper to taste

PREPARATION TIME: about 20 minutes

COOKING TIMES: about 40 minutes

EQUIPMENT YOU WILL NEED

Saucepan - Chopping board - Chopping knife

Strainer - Fork

METHOD STOVETOP

Boil the diced eggplant for about half an hour. When they are ready you can see that they are a medium brown. Allow to drain and use a fork to press them down until all the water has drained from them. Allow to cool for at least an hour.

You can place them into a food processor or do this with your hands. I usually squish them until they look mushy and then add all the other ingredients. I allow them to sit for about 20 minutes before tossing them again and then serve. I also taste them to see if there is any more oil or vinegar to add for more flavour.

ESSENTIAL SECRET INGREDIENTS

Make this dish with your grandmother or someone who is a mentor that you admire

Have plenty of conversation

Drink a glass of Italian Marsala with plenty of love

PEPERONI ROSTITI CON MELANZANI (ROASTED PEPPERS AND EGGPLANTS)

My mother Sarina's recipe

Serves 2

INGREDIENTS

- 2 red capsicums
- 1 eggplant
- 1 brown onion
- Fresh oregano
- 1 crushed clove of garlic
- Virgin olive oil
- salt/pepper

PREPARATION TIME: about 15 minutes

COOKING TIME: about 30 minutes

METHOD: GRILL/OVEN/BBQ

Wash the capsicums, eggplant and onion and place under the grill. Cook until they are soft and ready to peel. It will take about half an hour. When the capsicums are ready, my mother taught me to put them into a plastic bag. That makes them sweat and the skin comes off easily. Leave them for about half an hour.

Remove the meat from the eggplant with a spoon, leaving the skin as you don't eat that and cut the brown onion into small chunks, placing them into a bowl. Then peel the skin from the red capsicums and dice the meat. Gently add fresh oregano, crushed garlic, salt/pepper and virgin olive oil and toss.

TIP: This is a side dish we often eat with either our cotolettas or as a summer meal with a loaf of fresh bread.

SALMON CARPACCIO

SERVES 2

INGREDIENTS

- 200g fresh smoked salmon
- 1 tablespoon baby capers (drained)
- Virgin olive oil
- Cracked pepper
- Fresh dill chopped

PREPARATION TIME: about 10 minutes

METHOD BENCHTOP

Place the smoked salmon onto a serving plate. Place the capers and cracked pepper on top. Drizzle with virgin olive oil and fresh dill and serve.

You can even add a red onion if you like. The flavours burst onto your palate.

You need to eat fresh bread or ciabatta with this. It's great for a spuntini/primo piatti.

TIP: If you don't like the taste of capers, you can rinse them in running water which removes the vinegar taste.

OLIVE FRITTI (FRIED OLIVES)

Carmela's Cucina Povera recipe

SERVES 2

INGREDIENTS

- 500g black maranatha olives
- 1 sprig rosemary
- 1 sprig lemon thyme
- 4 fresh sage leaves
- 1 clove garlic
- 1 small sliced fresh chilli
- Lemon rind (grated)
- Olive oil

PREPARATION TIME: about 15 minutes

Cooking time: about 10 minutes

EQUIPMENT YOU WILL NEED

Small frying pan

Wooden spoon

METHOD STOVETOP

Place all the ingredients into a small frying pan and let them sizzle for about 5 minutes, allowing the flavours to enrich the olives. Constantly toss them around in the pan with a wooden spoon. Place the olives onto a plate and serve with fresh bread.

VEGETABLE DISHES

It's just a part of who we are!............

ESSENTIAL SECRET INGREDIENTS
Warmth, love, happy, gratitude and smiles.

Vegetables are so important. You automatically feel better when you eat them. They contain such healing agents. You think more clearly. Sicilians love their verdure (greens) and grow them in their gardens. As with any Sicilian/Italian, it's just a part of who we are. Without our verdura, it's like having no oxygen in our blood, it's just not possible.

Here are just a few recipes that I have made through the years that my mother and grandmother also used to make. I have simply added more texture, as I love flavour. All of my recipes involve seasonal produce from organic farms or local farmers as they create the taste sensations and are healthier.

SECARI CON PATATI (SILVERBEET WITH POTATOES)

Carmela's Cucina Povera recipe

SERVES 2

INGREDIENTS

- 1 bunch of silverbeet cleaned and cut into small pieces
- 1 large purple sweet potato
- 1 bunch broccoli
- 1 clove garlic (crushed)
- Virgin olive oil
- Salt/pepper to taste
- Add ½ a chilli when you are frying the garlic if you desire.

PREPARATION TIME: about 20 minutes

COOKING TIME: about 30 minutes

EQUIPMENT YOU WILL NEED

Aldi Frying pan - Strainer - Wooden spoon

Chopping board - Chopping knife - Large saucepan

METHOD STOVETOP

Fill a saucepan with water and bring to the boil. Add the silverbeet and cook for about 15 minutes. Then add the potato and broccoli. When they are cooked, strain and reheat. In a frying pan add the crushed garlic clove with virgin olive oil. Allow to sizzle, add the remaining ingredients and stir. If you need to, add more oil then serve with your favourite meat or cottoletta.

TIP: I always use a purple sweet potato, as they become very mushy and add texture to the verdura.

BROCCOLI RAPPI

My mother Sarina's recipe

SERVES 2

INGREDIENTS

- 1 bunch Broccoli Rappi
- 1 garlic clove (crushed)
- Virgin olive oil
- ½ chilli (diced)

PREPARATION TIME: about 15 minutes

COOKING TIME: about 45 minutes

EQUIPMENT YOU WILL NEED

Strainer

Chopping board

Chopping knife

Cooking pot

Frying pan

METHOD STOVETOP

Place water into a saucepan and bring to the boil. Add the Broccoli Rappi and allow to cook. They usually take about 30 to 40 minutes, then, drain. Add virgin olive oil, garlic and chilli to a frying pan, allowing it to sizzle and become golden brown. Then add the cooked Broccoli Rappi and fry for about 3 minutes. Serve with your favourite side dish and fresh bread.

TIP: I usually eat Rappi with veal cotolettas.

NOTE: Rappi needs cleaning and you have to make sure that they are washed thoroughly. I usually rinse them about 4 times.

Rappi is a green vegetable that many Italians grow in their garden. You find it at your local market and most fruit vendors.

These are my favourites. My father used to grow them in the garden just for his Carmelusa. Oh, how I miss his face coming down my street with all of the vegetables from his garden.
His face was so happy when he brought them to me.

ZUCCHINI FRITTELLI

Carmela's Cucina Povera recipe

SERVES 2

INGREDIENTS

- 500g zucchini (grated)
- 4 zucchini flowers, cleaned and diced
- ½ carrot (grated)
- 1 cup Pecorino cheese (grated)
- 3 eggs (beaten)
- 1/4 cup flour for binding
- Sea salt and pepper for seasoning
- Freshly torn basil leaves

PREPARATION TIME: about 20 minutes

COOKING TIME: about 15 minutes

EQUIPMENT YOU WILL NEED

Ceramic bowl - Wooden spoon - Aldi Frying pan - Grater

Whisk - Medium chopping board - Medium chopping knife

METHOD STOVETOP

Combine all ingredients in a mixing bowl and mix well using a wooden spoon. Heat the oil in a pan. When the oil is hot, measure a tablespoonful of the mixture and place in the heated oil. Continue until mixture is used up - just like making frittelli or polpetti.

Cook for about 3 to 4 minutes until they are golden, turn them over and cook for a further 3 to 4 minutes. Then, place each piece onto a serving plate with kitchen paper to drain the excess oil. They're great to serve as starters.

- -

CARMELA'S CUCINA POVERA RECIPE FOR ZUCCHINI FRITTI

SERVES 2

This is a simple dish of Cucina Povera. Once again it so simple but the taste is amazing.

INGREDIENTS

- ½ kg seasonal organic zucchini (cubed)
- Olive oil for frying
- Sea salt and cracked pepper
- Romano cheese (grated)
- Freshly torn basil

PREPARATION TIME: about 15 minutes

COOKING TIME: about 15 minutes

EQUIPMENT YOU WILL NEED

Medium sauté pan - Wooden spoon - Medium chopping board

Medium chopping knife

METHOD STOVETOP

Heat the oil in a medium sauté pan. Add the zucchini, turning them occasionally and cook until they are golden brown. When cooked, place onto a serving plate. Add sea salt and cracked pepper, basil, grated Romano cheese and serve with veal/chicken/pork cotolettas.

Frittelli means
'little fried things'.

TIP: They need to be moist.
The mixture must be made close to runny. When you eat them they need to be soft inside, so with this recipe practice makes perfect.

EQUIPMENT ESSENTIALS

EQUIPMENT ESSENTIALS

I recommend that you buy your equipment from a local Italian importer. There are many places that you can get them. Even Italian supermarkets stock all types of machinery that is needed for these dishes.

A local importer in Melbourne is www.costanteimports.com.au.

WHAT YOU NEED TO BUY

When you have some spare change, you can buy most of these items at Aldi when they are in stock. Usually every few months they have good quality frying pans, sausage machines, food processors and mixers on sale, so don't go over your budget and overspend.

> Sausage funnel or sausage machine
> Large, medium, small frying pans from Aldi with lids
> A good quality knife for chopping either medium/large - you can get them at Woolworths
> A paring knife
> A small/medium/large chopping board
> Pizza stone
> Italian Passatutto machine
> Food processor
> A good quality ceramic bowl
> A flat biscuit tray for baking
> Cheese grater
> Flour sifter
> Crock pot
> Heavy sauté pan
> Casserole pot
> Pizza trays

USING THE BEST INGREDIENTS

Experience in cooking for me has been a journey of knowing what blends well with each recipe and each ingredient.

PASTA BRANDS I RECOMMEND

Barilla Pasta is one that you can never go wrong with. In saying that, Divella and Grana Padano pasta are also great names with good reputations behind them. There are many types available and you can easily get confused so I stick to what I know.

Gluten-free pasta for me has always been either Barilla or San Remo. Another brand with a wide range is BioFood Organic Gluten Free. This pasta keeps and holds its own and does not break or separate.

Romanella, imported by Corecco Fine Foods, is made up of 80 per cent cornflour and 20 per cent rice flour.

I developed food intolerances in my forties and have substituted gluten-free pasta, bread and rice for my meals. If I am making meatballs (I have a great recipe that makes the best meatballs) and need breadcrumbs, I use multigrain gluten-free bread that is usually stale. I make the breadcrumbs then soak them in milk for about half an hour then drain. I also use Zymil milk, as I am lactose intolerant.

BRANDS OF DICED TOMATOES I RECOMMEND

There are a lot of different diced tomato brands out there but I like to stick with what I know – companies like Divella and Sole Natura. These companies have a great reputation for using fresh tomatoes.

CHOOSING YOUR CHEESES

Pecorino is one of my favourites, as I love the bite it has. I also love Romano which is very good for you. I also found that it doesn't contain the enzyme that causes me to bloat. Pecorino and Romano are the two cheeses that I like to grate for cooking because of their flavour.

Parmesan is also great for cooking with and coating cottolettas, if you don't have either of the other two.

CHOOSING ORGANIC, MARKET-FRESH INGREDIENTS

With Cucina Povera, I only use organic market-fresh ingredients.

WHY BUYING FRESH MATTERS

We only get one body and one shot at living, so let's give it our best, each day that we wake up. What we don't get the chance to do today we can do tomorrow. It's about getting into a routine. It soon becomes a way of life.

Always use fresh ingredients as the flavour stays in the food for days. Always choose reputable brands – brands that have stood the test of time usually offer consistent product quality.

Market-fresh ingredients from your local greengrocer or market, is important because you know by choosing them that they are fresh and brought to the store every day.

Living on the Mornington Peninsula, I am a bit spoilt, as we have a market every week with local farmers we can buy from. I do buy groceries from the local supermarket, but only when I am pressed for time!

You can source your meat from the local butcher shop, your fresh seafood from the local fish shop and your eggs from a local farmer.

VALUE YOU

Your body is like a prestige car. Food is fuel. What we put into our bodies is very important as it helps them to run smoothly and efficiently. Of course you should make sure you give your body a regular service and check-up. You are the most important person in the world. Invest in yourself and eat food that will help you through the day to work efficiently. Life today is so fast-paced that it's important that we each spend that little bit of extra time eating healthily.

SLOW DOWN AND SAVOUR IT

If we stop when we eat and take the time to listen to our body and our senses, they tell us to eat slowly and chew more. Making this style of eating part of our daily regime, we will have a better digestive system.

HOW TO TAKE CARE OF YOUR BODY

> - Listen to your body
> - Eat slowly
> - Chew more
> - Take more time and care with food.

When you are having a quiet cup of coffee, prepare your shopping list and put it in your diary. Then you can just pop by and do a little shop. Soon you will become more organised and regain your power over your health.

HOW TO GET STARTED: PLANNING ESSENTIALS

There is an old saying that if you don't plan you will fail, so you need to plan to not fail. For me, planning is a must. Without a diary my brain will explode. I can't keep everything I have to do in my head.

Planning your week – what you are going to buy and cook – makes a big difference to your health. Take it slow and steady. Chi va piano va sano e va lontano – he who goes slow and steady goes a long way.

When I'm cooking I also need to plan, because if I don't and I go and do the shopping, I end up buying things that I don't need and throwing them out. And I end up throwing money and time out. For me, planning is non-negotiable. Otherwise, I might as well throw money down the toilet and end up eating rubbish, with little time to cook.

MY DAILY ESSENTIALS

> Waking up and feeling gratitude
> An hour's walk
> An hour's writing time
> Making sure I eat nutritional food
> Spending 15 minutes in the sun in the morning

MY WEEK AT A GLANCE: NINE STRATEGIES FOR SAVING TIME, MONEY AND STRESS

1. Planning the week
2. Planning meals
3. Planning where I will shop and buy my groceries, meat and vegetables
4. Planning my daily routine
5. Attending appointments (dentist, chiropractor, etc.)
6. Social planning: visiting friends or family
7. Planning family time: making time for my husband, my children and having lunch with them
8. Planning my day off and having fun
9. Switching my phone off and returning missed calls (I come from a generation when there were no mobile phones so it is not a necessity).

WAYS TO HAVE FUN WITH FOOD PREPARATION

- Wear a pretty apron
- Lay a tablecloth on the table (or placemats)
- Add wine glasses with a great Sicilian wine and having a glass (only one) while you cook.
- Play music that you love
- Plan your meals
- Pre-make meals and freeze them.

HOW TO MAKE GREAT PIZZA DOUGH

Making a pizza from scratch requires a simple process. You can create a pizza just the way you like it by adding your favourite toppings. Most people believe that Italians invented pizza, but its origin goes back to ancient times in the Middle East. Babylonians, Israelites, Egyptians, Armenians, Greeks and Romans plus many other cultures ate flat, unleavened bread cooked in mud ovens. The ancient Greeks, Romans and Egyptians were eating bread topped with olive oil and spices, which today is called focaccia. They say that Raffaele Esposito from Naples was a baker who created the first pizza for the visit of King Umberto and Queen Margherita in Italy in 1889. He created it using the Italian colours of the flag, red being tomatoes, white being cheese and green being basil. The first pizza shop was the Port Alba in Naples, which opened in 1830 and is still open today.

Making a pizza from scratch requires a simple process. You can create a pizza just the way you like it by adding your favourite toppings.

PIZZA DOUGH

My mother Sarina's recipe, updated by Carmela

Makes between 2-3 large 12-inch pizzas

INGREDIENTS

- 25g fresh yeast
- 1 and 1/2 cups warm water
- 1 teaspoon sugar
- 2 tablespoons olive oil
- 3 and a 1/4 cups 00 flour
- ½ cup plain flour (White Wings)
- 2 teaspoons salt
- Your choice of toppings

PREPARATION TIME: about 30 minutes

COOKING TIME: about 40 to 50 minutes

Preheat a 200°C oven for 30 minutes

EQUIPMENT YOU WILL NEED

Pizza stone

Wooden spoons

Spatulas

Ceramic mixing bowl

12 inch pizza pan

TIP: Use the White Wings Plain Flour for dusting.

METHOD OVEN

In a large mixing bowl, add the fresh yeast to 1 1/2 cups of warm water. Wait 2 to 3 minutes for the yeast to rise. Mix in 1/2 a cup of plain flour and a teaspoon of sugar. Be sure to mix it well.

Next, add 2 tablespoons of olive oil, 2 teaspoons of salt, gradually adding 3 1/4 cups of 00 flour. Work the ingredients together, using your hands or a large wooden spoon.

Transfer the dough to a smooth, flour-dusted surface and knead until the dough is smooth. This should take about 5 minutes. If the dough becomes sticky when you're kneading it, gradually add extra flour (up to another 1/4 of a cup).

Place the dough into a large bowl that's been lightly greased with olive oil. Cover the bowl and allow the dough to double in size. Place it somewhere warm, as dough rises better when it is in a warm place. This should take about an hour.

Divide the dough into two pieces and roll each piece into balls. Rest the dough for 15 minutes on the bench, covered with a tea towel. >>>>

Then place a ball of dough onto a floured counter or work surface and flatten with your hands. Keep stretching and pressing down on the dough until it reaches the desired size of a large pizza approximately 12 inches wide.

Slide your hands underneath the dough and lift it onto an oiled pizza pan. Depending on the size and shape of your dough, you may also use a baking sheet.

Before placing your toppings on the dough see the tip below under 'toppings'.

Toppings on traditional Sicilian pizzas are generally light. We love to use fresh toppings, like sliced tomatoes, slices of Mozzarella, bocconcini, buffalo Mozzarella, anchovies and olives. The simpler, the better. I love to add fresh rocket, after the pizza is cooked, as it is nutritious.

Bake the pizza in a 200°C oven until the cheese and edge of the crust looks golden brown. If you have any doubts, carefully lift up the crust with a metal spatula (plastic can melt!) to see whether the bottom of the crust is lightly browned.

TOPPINGS FOR HEALTHY PIZZAS

TIP: Making a pizza takes practice and a lot of knowledge. It's not as simple as you think. My advice is to brush a little olive oil on the dough before you do anything else and when you cook your pizza, always cook it for half the time in the oven, then add your toppings and return it to the oven.

If you have planned your menu for the week, you can pre-cook the dough and store it in the fridge for a few days or freeze it to make life even easier.

ESSENTIAL SECRET INGREDIENTS

Love, patience, warmth, a glass of aperitivo, an Italian apron and some fluffy slippers!

This is one of my favourite creations, I call it Pizza della Signora.

PIZZA DELLA SIGNORA

Carmela's Cucina Povera recipe

SERVES 2

INGREDIENTS

- 1 tomato (sliced)
- 1 cup Mozzarella cheese
- 1 cup feta cheese (diced)
- 2 cups rocket
- ½ cup semi sundried tomatoes
- 3 leaves of freshly torn basil

PREPARATION TIME: about 20 minutes

COOKING TIME: about 30 minutes

Preheat a 200°C oven for 30 minutes

EQUIPMENT YOU WILL NEED:

Pizza stone

Medium chopping board

Medium chopping knife

METHOD: oven/pizza stone/wood-fired oven

Place your pre-cooked pizza on a pizza tray, adding fresh tomatoes, Mozzarella cheese and fresh basil. Place in the oven for around 15 minutes. Once the pizza is cooked, cut into 6 slices and top with feta cheese and rocket. Drizzle a little virgin olive oil on top and there you go.

I use market-fresh ingredients when I make this, as the flavours tend to burst in your mouth. This meal is so nutritious and healthy.

GIARDINA DEL GIARDINO

Carmela's Cucina Povera recipe

SERVES 2

INGREDIENTS

- 1 zucchini, sliced lengthways
- 1 potato (sliced)
- 2 red capsicums
- 4 freshly torn basil leaves
- ½ cup cherry tomatoes
- ½ cup Mozzarella cheese
- 2 tablespoons tomato paste
- Ingredients for pizza dough or pre-cooked pizza base

PREPARATION TIME: about 20 minutes

COOKING TIME: about 40 minutes

Preheat a 200°C oven for 30 minutes

EQUIPMENT YOU WILL NEED

Oven tray - Pizza stone - Greaseproof paper - Plastic bag

Ceramic bowl - Wooden spoon

METHOD OVEN/BENCHTOP

Place the red capsicums on a tray with greaseproof paper in the oven to cook on a high temperature. This takes about half an hour. They're ready when the skin is black and the meat of the capsicums looks like it is peeling. Remove from the oven and allow them to sit while you prepare the other ingredients.

Prepare your pizza dough. Place it on your pizza tray and allow it to sit and rest which allows the dough to slowly rise. Dough needs its own time. If you do this, you will find that you have created a light texture and it will be crunchy on the outside and soft in the inside.

You can either grill the zucchini (a healthy alternative) or fry it. The same goes for the potatoes. Peel the skin off the capsicums and place them on a plate. Now you are ready to start to make your masterpiece.

Place your pizza dough (or pre-cooked pizza base) onto a pizza tray and add some tomato paste – just a little to moisten the top – followed by half of the Mozzarella cheese, the zucchini, potatoes, red capsicums, cherry tomatoes, fresh basil and adding the remaining Mozzarella on top.

Place the pizza in the oven, allowing it to cook for about half an hour. Check it regularly. Serve with a salad and you have a nutritious meal.

TIP: When I serve this one I also like to put some buffalo bocconcini on top and drizzle with some virgin olive oil

PIZZA CON CARCIOFI (ARTICHOKES)

Carmela's Cucina Povera recipe

INGREDIENTS

1 pre-cooked pizza base.
1½ cups Mozzarella
2 cups marinated carciofi (artichokes)
Oregano
2 tomatoes thinly cut
½ cup goats' cheese
Olive oil
Salt/pepper to taste

PREPARATION TIME: about 15 minutes

COOKING TIME: about 20 minutes

Preheated oven at 200°C for 15 minutes

EQUIPMENT YOU WILL NEED

Pizza tray

Chopping board

Chopping knife

METHOD OVEN

Place your pre-cooked pizza base onto a pizza tray. Brush with olive oil then add the tomato slices, Mozzarella, carciofi, oregano and salt/pepper. Cook in a preheated oven at 200°C for about 15 minutes. Check it regularly. Place the pizza onto a serving plate, adding goats' cheese, a sprinkle of virgin olive oil and a little bit more fresh oregano. Cut and serve.

TIP: You can also add salami to this, as well as olives and freshly sliced tomatoes.

ROCCI DEL MARE (SEAFOOD PIZZA)

Carmela's Cucina Povera recipe

SERVES 2
INGREDIENTS

- 4 king prawns
- 1 fresh fish (diced)
- 2 pieces fresh calamari (thinly sliced)
- 6 fresh mussels
- 6 clams
- ½ cup parsley (chopped) with 2 tablespoons of olive oil (mix together with the fresh chilli)
- 1 garlic clove (crushed)
- Virgin olive oil
- ½ fresh chilli
- 4 basil leaves
- 1 cup Mozzarella (grated)
- Salt/pepper to taste
- Ingredients for pizza dough or pre-cooked pizza base

PREPARATION TIME: about 20 minutes

COOKING TIME: about 15 minutes

Preheat a 200°C oven for 30 minutes

EQUIPMENT YOU WILL NEED

Pizza stone

Pizza trays

Frying pan

Ceramic bowl

Medium chopping board

Medium chopping knife

Paring knife

METHOD OVEN

Make your pizza dough. Let it sit and rise while you prepare your pizza ingredients. When ready cook it for half the time in the oven.

Place the oil, garlic and parsley into a non-stick frying pan and let it sizzle and soak up the ingredients. Next, add the seafood, placing the lid on top of the pan. Allow the flavours to combine only for about 3 to 4 minutes. They need to be at least half cooked.

Remove the pan from the stove and let it cool down. Place the virgin olive oil, garlic and chilli paste on the pizza base, followed by the seafood, basil leaves and Mozzarella.

Add the ingredients to your pizza base and bake in the oven, checking it regularly. It won't take long if you have pre-cooked the base.

TIP: Always use fresh herbs when you are about to serve this pizza, as the flavours remain and absorb into the pizza, and drizzle virgin olive oil on top.

> The sea, once it casts its spell, holds one in its net of wonder forever.
>
> ……………………… Jacques Yves Cousteau

COOKING WITH FRESH HERBS

I LOVE HERBS.

They are as part of the universe, as are the trees and the stars. In them you can find a sweet aroma to life.

I have a few herbs growing in the garden and every year I try to build up my supply, but to no avail, because my son Joseph's dog, Payne, an English Staffy decides that he always wants to play in my garden. So each year I have to start all over again!

Having a herb garden is also very therapeutic. Nature allows you to heal and to be still. I find that I feel in tune with the earth when I am pottering around in the garden. It's when time is my friend and I love it. Everything in life is good when I am in my garden.

Fresh herbs are used almost exclusively in Italian cooking because they taste better than dried herbs. Fresh herbs contain aromatic oils. The intensity of herbs vary, so when you must substitute them, try to pick something with a similar punch, or be prepared to adjust the amount you use.

ESSENTIAL SECRET INGREDIENTS

Smell each herb, listen from your soul about what each herb goes with. Be brave and try plenty of herbs. Drink a glass of Moscato and smile for the day.

HERBS USED IN SICILIAN COOKING

HERB	ITALIAN	DESCRIPTION
Basil	Basilico	Italy's best-known herb, basil has a strong anise flavour. A must in pesto, basil is a natural complement to tomatoes because its sweetness works nicely with the acidity in the tomatoes. Tarragon, which isn't widely used in Italy, has a similar anise flavour and can be used as a substitute. You can also use parsley in most recipes that call for basil.
Bay leaf	Alloro	Once sold only dried, this herb is increasingly available fresh as well. Dried leaves are often dropped into a pot of simmering beans or soup to impart their gentle aroma. You can use fresh leaves, which tend to be longer and thinner, in the same fashion.
Marjoram	Maggiorana	This herb is similar to oregano but is milder in flavour. Popular in the Riviera, marjoram is good with meats and seafood.
Mint	Menta	You can find hundreds of kinds of mint. Some are mild and sweet; others spicy and hot. Mint is used more in southern Italy and has an intensity and freshness similar to basil, which is perhaps the best substitute.
Oregano	Origano	This herb has a potent aroma and flavour that predominates in much southern Italian cooking and is commonly used with tomatoes.
Parsley	Prezzemolo	This herb is the unheralded star of Italian cooking. Basil may get all the attention, but parsley is more widely used. Flat-leaf varieties have a stronger flavour than the curly-leaf kind. You can cook parsley with garlic and onions in olive oil to form the flavour base of many dishes.
Rosemary	Rosmarino	As rosemary has a strong resinous (or pine) aroma and flavour, use it sparingly. The tough needles need time to soften and you shouldn't add it to dishes that you don't cook. Rosemary is a natural with potatoes, chicken, lamb and beef.
Sage	Salvia	Sage is especially popular in Tuscany and other parts of central and northern Italy. It is pungent, with a musty mint taste and works well in butter sauces, as well as with pork and chicken.
Thyme	Timo	Diminutive thyme leaves pack a surprising punch. Many varieties have a lemony flavour. Thyme isn't as widely used in Italy as other herbs, but lemon thyme is one of my favourites.

My favourite herbs are basil, rosemary, sage and thyme. I put them in just about everything that I cook. The smells make me want to stretch out to the earth and say thank you.

Dishes are given their character not by smothering them in sauces but by using top quality ingredients that complement one another. A true Sicilian cook would rather leave out an ingredient than add one.

At the moment Italy is the leading European country for organic farming. Some 50,000 farms or estates cultivate nearly one million hectares of land without the use of chemicals and use only organic fertilisers.

Italians always use seasonal produce. My father only ate what was in season and so did my nonno. Their garden was always blossoming with what was in season and the quality of the ingredients is what makes a meal. You can taste the freshness in every meal. That is what makes the dishes.

EXPLORING SICILIAN WINES

There is no meal in a Sicilian family that does not have wine at la tavola (the table).

We have many wines that are very popular. My favourite is Nero D'Avola, a hearty red with a full body. You can taste the berries. My favourite in Australia is a strong Black Tongue Shiraz.

A SNAPSHOT OF SICILY

Sicily is the largest island in the Mediterranean Sea. It is officially referred to as Regione Siciliana (Sicilian Region).

Sicily is located in the central Mediterranean. It extends from the tip of the Apennine peninsula, from which it is separated only by the narrow Strait of Messina, towards the North African coast. Its most prominent landmark is Mount Etna, which at 3,350 metres is the tallest active volcano in Europe and one of the most active in the world.

Sicily has many different cultural influences that range from the Greeks, Normans, Arabs, Spanish, French and many more. Following the expedition of the thousand, a Giuseppe Garibaldi-led revolt during the Italian Unification process, it became part of Italy in 1860. After the birth of the Italian Republic in 1946, Sicily was given special status as an autonomous region. Sicily has a rich and unique culture, especially with regard to the arts, music, literature, cuisine and architecture.

MY FATHER'S WINE

Every year my father made his own wine and every year he swore it was the best. He would trade it with his compares (best men, from weddings and baptisms) and friends of the family and they would compete against one another.

He stored wine in his shed for many years. Rather than throwing anything away they would make red wine vinegar. In his words, what he had was benedizione del dio (blessings from God).

I remember hearing about Sicily's history and the story of Salvatore Giuliano, while sitting at my father's feet listening to the record player. He would go so quiet and passionate at the same time. I could not understand what had happened to Sicily, as I was only a young girl in a new country, but he was so passionate about the unification and the freedom of Sicily. Salvatore Giuliano was like the Robin Hood of Sherwood Forest.

READ MORE ABOUT SALVATORE GUIILIANO HERE:

en.wikipedia.org/wiki/Salvatore_Giuliano

A FEW WINES FROM SICILY TO TRY

Here are a few wines from Sicily. There are many others made in Italy, that the country is famous for - like pinot grigio and chardonnay.

Carricante	A white wine from the Etna area.
Cataratto Bianco	A white traditional wine in the Trapani area and used in Marsala wine, characterised by delicate flavours and medium alcohol level.
Cianti	A light red wine that is used at any meal, not too much body, but delightful.
Corinto	A light white.
Gaglioppo	A red of Calabrian origin frequently grown in Sicily, similar to Frappato.
Grecanico (Greco)	A white, so-called for its Greek origins and genetically very similar to the garganega grown in Veneto.
Grillo	A distinctive white.
Inzolia, Insolia or Anzolia	Used to create dry white table wines as a blend with varieties such as chardonnay.
Malvasia	A muscatel sub-variety used to make the wine of this name, but the term more properly refers to the Moscato grape.
Moscato	Muscat, a traditional variety widely used in Italy. In Sicily it is associated with the dessert wine of this name, similar to Malvasia. The muscatels are one of European winemaking's most widespread grape types.
Nerello	A strong red grown in two varieties: Mascalese and Cappuccino.
Nero D'Avola	A hearty red used in some of Sicily's most popular wines.
Perricone	An esoteric, robust red.
Primitivo	Traditional red, probably Balkan in origin. It is rare in Sicily.
Zibibbo Moscatellone	A white possibly introduced into Sicily by the Saracen Arabs during the ninth century, it's used in fortified wines and is one of Sicily's muscatel mainstays.

There are so many to choose from! These are just a few wines. Of course, there are also liqueurs, aperitifs, grappas, Limoncello ...

KNOWING YOUR PASTA VARIETIES

What is important for me is knowing what makes me feel better after I have eaten. I have food intolerances and I know what is best for my health.

Knowing the constituents of what type of pasta to choose is important. For me, Barilla or Divella is great as it made from semolina or grando duro. I am often also asked which flour is the best.

I find that the Italian flour 00 is best to use. It's versatile – you can stretch it and work with it … really play with it.

THE HISTORY OF PASTA

Pasta is a staple food of traditional Italian cuisine, with the first reference to it dating from 1154 in Sicily.

It is also commonly used to refer to the variety of pasta dishes. Typically, pasta is a noodle made from unleavened dough of durum wheat flour mixed with water and formed into sheets or various shapes, then cooked and served in any number of dishes. It can be made with flour from other cereals or grains and eggs may be used instead of water.

Pastas may be divided into two broad categories: dried (pasta secca) and fresh (pasta fresca). Chicken eggs frequently dominate as the source of the liquid component in fresh pasta. Most dried pasta is commercially produced via an extrusion process. Fresh pasta was traditionally produced by hand, sometimes with the aid of simple machines. Today, many fresh pasta varieties are commercially produced by large-scale machines. The products are widely available in supermarkets.

Both dried and fresh pasta come in a number of shapes and varieties – there are more than 1300 different sorts: http://en.wikipedia.org/wiki/Pasta - cite_note-Zanini-4 .

In Italy, the names of specific pasta shapes or types often vary according to their locale. For example the form macaroni is known by different names depending on the region and town.

Common forms of pasta include long shapes, short shapes, tubes, flat shapes and sheets, miniature soup shapes, filled or stuffed and specialty or decorative shapes. As a category in Italian cuisine, both fresh and dried pastas are classically used in one of three kinds of prepared dishes.

As pasta asciutta (dry, or pastasciutta), cooked pasta is plated and served with a complementary sauce or condiment. A second classification of pasta dishes is pasta in brodo (soup) in which the pasta is part of a soup-type dish. A third category is pasta al forno (oven) in which the pasta is incorporated into a dish that is subsequently baked.

Pasta is generally a simple dish, but comes in many varieties because it is a versatile food. Some pasta dishes are served as a first course in Sicily/Italy because the portion sizes are small and simple.

Pasta is also used in light lunches, such as salads or in larger portion sizes for dinner. It can be prepared by hand or using a food processor and served hot or cold.

Pasta sauces vary in taste, colour and texture. When choosing which types of pasta and sauce to serve together, there is a general rule that must be observed. Simple sauces like pesto are ideal for long and thin strands of pasta while tomato sauce combines well with thicker pastas. Thicker and chunkier sauces have a better ability to cling onto the holes and cuts of short, tubular, twisted pastas. The ratio of sauce to pasta varies according to taste and texture, however traditionally the sauce should not be excessive, as the pasta itself must still be tasted. The extra sauce left on the plate after all of the pasta is eaten is often mopped up with a piece of bread

HERE IS A SMALL TABLE TO SHOW YOU WHAT BLENDS WELL.

COMBINING PASTA TYPES WITH SAUCES

Spaghetti	Oil base, Napoli, cream, Bolognese
Macaroni/penne/rigatoni	Napoli, oil, cream
Fusilli	Napoli, oil
Linguini	Oil, Napoli
Ravioli/tortellini	Oil, butter, Napoli, cream, Bolognese, soups
Strozzapiedi	Napoli
Pappardelle	Napoli, stofado (stew)

Pastas come in an amazing variety of shapes. Certain Sicilian/Italian dishes call for specific pasta shapes because they complement the sauce.

PRE-COOKING PASTA

Here is a great tip and advice for the busy person who is pressed for time. I pre-cook my pasta if I am really busy and don't have time to spare. I boil the quantity that I need in salted water, usually allowing about 125g per person, but cook for about half the time that it is required to fully cook it.

Then I drain the pasta and place it onto a flat baking tray and toss with a little olive oil. Next, place it in the fridge for about 10 minutes to cool. I keep tossing it around so that it doesn't stick. When it has cooled, I place it on the bench and roll it into a 125g portion for each serve and store in an airtight container. It will keep for about 4 days.

You can use gluten-free pasta and any other type that you like.

COMMON PASTA SHAPES

Agnolotti:	Filled fresh pasta shaped like half moons.
Bucatini:	Long, fat strands that look like spaghetti but are hollow like little tubes.
Capelli d'angelo:	Long and extremely thin. Name translates as angel's hair.
Cappellini:	Slightly thicker than angel hair pasta but still very thin, long strands.
Conchiglie:	Shell-shaped pasta that comes in a variety of sizes. Oversized shells, called conchiglioni, are often stuffed and baked.
Ditali:	Tiny tubes often used in soup. Name translates as thimbles.
Farfalle:	Bow-tie-shaped pasta. Name translates as butterflies.
Fettuccine:	Long, flat strands of egg noodles.
Fusilli:	Corkscrew shapes that come in varying lengths.
Lasagna:	Long, wide sheets of pasta that are layered with sauce and cheese and baked.
Linguine:	Long, thin ribbons. Similar to spaghetti except strands have flat sides as well as rounded ones.
Orecchiette:	Small bowl-shaped pasta. Name translates as little ears.
Orzo:	Shaped like extra long grains of rice. Often used in soup.
Pappardelle:	Long, flat noodle that is two to three times as wide as fettuccine. Often cut into shorter pieces for ease of eating.
Pastina:	Any of the tiny pasta added to soup, including ditalini (little thimbles), perline (little pearls) and stelline (little stars).
Penne:	Medium-length tubes with ends cut on an angle. Can be ridged. Name translates as quills.
Ravioli:	Stuffed pasta shaped like square pillows. Edges are often ruffled.
Rigatoni:	Fat, squat tubes with grooved exterior.
Rotelle:	Small wheels.
Ruote:	Wheels.
Spaghetti:	Long, thin strands. Name comes from the word spago, meaning string or cord.
Strozzapiedi:	An elongated form of cavatelli or hand-rolled pasta typical of the Emilia-Romagna, Tuscany, Marche and Umbria regions of Italy. These are great with Napoli. The name translates as priest-strangler!
Tagliatelle:	Long, flat strands that are slightly wider than fettuccine.
Taglierini:	Similar to tagliatelle but cut narrower.
Tortellini:	Stuffed pasta shaped like fat rings. Often used in soups.
Trenette:	A long-strand pasta shape that is similar to linguine.
Vermicelli:	Long, very thin strands which are thinner than spaghetti. Name translates as little worms.
Ziti:	Narrow tubes of medium length. Similar to penne except the ends are not cut on an angle.

CUCINA POVERA RECIPES FOR PASTA

I cannot ever remember not eating pasta, or visiting a family member and not having pasta at the table.
Sicilians love their pasta and its origins go way back.

I have a story that I remember my mother-in-law Giuseppina telling me when my brother-in-law Eugene, God bless his soul, passed away. He was eating broken spaghetti at three months old, right up until he passed away. He always wanted a plate of pasta. He would refuse everything else, but not pasta!

ESSENTIAL SECRET INGREDIENTS

Family, love and conversation, smiles, tarantella Siciliana (Sicilian music) and a glass of Chianti

PESTO

Carmela's Cucina Povera recipe

SERVES 2

INGREDIENTS

- 2 cups cream
- 1 cup pesto
- 1 cup ricotta
- 8 butterflied king prawns
- 2 tablespoons virgin olive oil
- ½ cup Parmesan cheese (grated)
- Salt/pepper to taste

PREPARATION TIME: about 20 minutes

COOKING TIME: about 10 minutes

EQUIPMENT YOU WILL NEED

Aldi large frying pan - Medium chopping board

Medium chopping knife - Wooden spoon

Paring knife - Strainer

METHOD STOVETOP

Place the oil in a frying pan with the king prawns on a low heat. When the prawns are cooked, (you can see that they turn a red/orange colour) add the cream, pesto and ricotta. Stir the ingredients until the mixture acquires a medium to thick consistency.

Add your favourite pasta to this sauce. I recommend spaghetti, penne/rigatoni or pappardelle.

TIP: You can even make risotto with this recipe.

PASTA AL TONNO (TUNA)

Carmela's Cucina Povera recipe

SERVES 2

INGREDIENTS

> 1 fresh tuna steak or 185g tin of tuna (Sirena brand)
> 1 cup cherry tomatoes
> 1 tablespoon dill (thinly sliced)
> 1 tablespoon basil (thinly sliced)
> 1 tablespoon baby capers
> 1 tablespoon lemon rind
> 1 cup rocket
> ½ cup black pitted olives (kalamata, as they maintain their consistency when cooking)
> 250g pre-cooked pasta (such as penne or fusilli) I always use the gluten-free pasta
> Extra virgin olive oil
> Grated Pecorino or Romano
> You can also add fresh chilli to your required taste. I usually add about 1 teaspoon while I am cooking.

PREPARATION TIME: about 20 minutes
COOKING TIME: about 10 minutes

EQUIPMENT YOU WILL NEED

Stainless steel bowl - Aldi medium frying pan - Paring knife

Medium chopping board - Medium chopping knife

Wooden spoon - Strainer - Cooking pot - Cheese grater

METHOD STOVETOP

Place all the ingredients into a stainless steel bowl so that when your pasta is ready you can add it to the bowl.

Place a pot containing around 3 litres of water onto the heat and bring to the boil. Add a pinch of salt, followed by your favourite pasta and cook for around 8 to 10 minutes depending on the type of pasta you are using.

Drain the pasta and toss with the ingredients to combine. Add a little bit of extra virgin olive oil, grate some fresh Pecorino or Romano cheese, place on a serving plate and mangia!

There are two ways to prepare this dish. You can make it as a warm salad, or heat the ingredients in a frypan then add the cooked pasta and stir. Once the ingredients have mixed thoroughly you can serve it.

ROCCI DEL MARE (ROCKS OF THE SEA)

SERVES 2

INGREDIENTS

- 6 king prawns
- 10 fresh mussels
- 2 scallops
- 4 clams
- 1 fresh fish (diced). Choose your preferred fish that keeps its firmness. You can even use flathead fillets.
- 2 garlic cloves (crushed)
- Virgin olive oil
- ½ cup parsley
- 250g pre-cooked pasta

PREPARATION TIME: about 20 minutes

COOKING TIME: about 20 minutes

EQUIPMENT YOU WILL NEED

Large frying pan

Chopping board

Paring knife

Stainless steel scourer

Chopping knife

Strainer

METHOD STOVETOP

Place the oil, garlic and half of the parsley into a frying pan and cook for about 2 minutes. Then add the seafood to the pan. Cook on a medium heat with the lid on, for about 4 minutes, the mussels will open up and have sweated. You will find that the seafood has a lot of water and it will become like a stew. Don't worry, because when you add the pasta, it will soak up the liquid.

I recommend using pappardelle, linguini or spaghetti. Add the pasta and extra parsley and a little more oil, allowing the flavours to develop. You will see that the pasta is omida (moist). Don't let it become dry. You can even add a little of the water from the pasta that you cooked.

Remember, you don't have to follow my instructions to the letter – you can add your own touches to each recipe.

My recipe gives you the foundation for Marinara, Rocci del Mare, Pescatore and Fruitto del Mare. You can add a little cream, or a little Napoli or even cherry tomatoes.

The versatility of this meal is amazing. You can have fresh bread at the table and make a beautiful salad and you have won your guests – or even your partner.

I love the Fruitto del Mare, which means fruits of the ocean. How poetic is that! Sicilians like to combine words like ingredients in a sauce.

··

There are many names for this dish, including Marinara, Pescatore and Fruitto del Mare. You can make an oil-based or cream-based Marinara. Pescatore is tomato-based and Fruitto del Mare is Napoli-based, with all kinds of seafood in the pasta.

I will give you the oil-based marinara dish as this is a benchmark for any seafood dish.

Pasta is such a flexible ingredient. I play with it all the time, to find the best way to work with it. If you're short on time, half cook the pasta, allow it to drain, place it on a flat tray, add just enough oil to coat it and toss it around. Place it in the fridge to cool and then remove and toss it around again to loosen it up and make a serving like a ball with your hands. You can even twist it. All it takes is a little practice. Cover the pasta with cling wrap and it will last for days.

CARBONARA

There are many ways to make this dish which is why I included the Fusion section in this book (see page 163). I've found that the old way and the new way of preparing these dishes have made a blend of their very own.

In the Australian version of Carbonara we use bacon, while in the Italian version we use pancetta. And in the Aussie/American version cream is used to give it more flavour and prevent it from being dry. However cream is not used in the Italian version, where oil and butter are the base of this sauce
plus egg yolks.

All these beautiful ingredients have been introduced to the old dishes over time, helping to unify them and to give them a new identity for the next generation to enjoy.

CARBONARA, SICILIAN/ITALIAN STYLE

SERVES 2

INGREDIENTS

- 2 strips pancetta (diced)
- 2 egg yolks
- ½ cup spring onions (finely chopped)
- 2 tablespoons butter
- 2 tablespoons virgin olive oil
- 1 garlic clove (chopped)
- ½ cup Parmesan cheese
- Pre-cooked pasta

PREPARATION TIME: about 20 minutes

COOKING TIME: about 15 minutes

EQUIPMENT YOU WILL NEED

Medium frying pan - Wooden spoon

Medium chopping board - Medium chopping knife

METHOD STOVETOP

Place the oil, butter and garlic into a frying pan, allowing it to sizzle for a few minutes. Next, add the spring onions and pancetta and cook for about 3 to 4 minutes until they brown. Add the cooked pasta to this mixture. The Sicilians love bugatini or little holes – like spaghetti with tubes in it – as it holds the oil and the flavours. Using a fresh pan, add the egg yolks and Parmesan cheese and toss around, on a low heat. Check whether the dish needs extra oil or butter then add to the pasta mixture. The Sicilians have this meal with a lot of oil and butter. And there you have your traditional Carbonara!

CARMELA'S CUCINA POVERA MATRICIANA

SERVES 2

INGREDIENTS

- 2 strips long rind bacon
- 1 cup spring onions diced
- 1 red capsicum (diced)
- Virgin olive oil
- Olives
- 4 basil leaves (sliced)
- ½ tablespoon garlic (finely chopped)
- ½ tablespoon fresh chilli
- 3 big ladles of cooked Napoli sauce page 127
- Fresh Parmesan/Romano cheese
- Pre-cooked pasta

PREPARATION TIME: about 20 minutes

COOKING TIME: about 15 minutes

EQUIPMENT YOU WILL NEED

Medium chopping board - Medium chopping knife

Medium frying pan - Wooden spoon

METHOD STOVETOP

Place the bacon, spring onions and red capsicum into a frying pan, together with the oil and allow to cook and brown on a high to medium heat, for about 4 minutes. Then add the Napoli sauce, olives, basil, chilli and garlic and allow to cook for another 3 minutes.

Add your favourite pasta to this sauce and sprinkle fresh Parmesan/Romano and serve with a beautiful salad. The best salad to have with this dish is Insalata di Marco.

SICILIAN LASAGNE

Carmela's Cucina Povera recipe

SERVES 4

INGREDIENTS

- 250g packet dry lasagne sheets (pre-boiled and placed in a tray with cold water and oil)
- 5 boiled eggs (grated)
- Béchamel sauce (see page 122 for recipe)
- Grated Mozzarella cheese
- Parmesan cheese
- 250g boiled peas
- About 10 cups of Bolognaise sauce (see page 122 for recipe)

PREPARATION TIME: about 50 minutes

COOKING TIME: about 50 minutes

Preheat a 200°C oven for 20 minutes

EQUIPMENT YOU WILL NEED

Oven tray - Cooking pot - Medium chopping board

Medium chopping knife - Saucepan

Rectangular or square oven dish

METHOD OVEN

Lightly grease the oven dish with butter. Add one ladle's worth of Bolognese sauce and a ladle of Béchamel sauce as a base.

Next, place lasagna sheets on top of the sauce so that they cover the dish, followed by a ladle of Bolognese sauce and a ladle of Béchamel sauce. Sprinkle a handful of peas, a grated egg, Mozzarella and Parmesan cheese and continue to build layers with the lasagne until there is no mixture remaining.

On the final layer, you need Bolognaise, Béchamel sauce, peas, grated egg, Mozzarella cheese and Parmesan cheese.

Place in a 200°C oven and cook for about 40 to 45 minutes, until the top is golden brown.

TIP: I usually make the Bolognaise sauce the day before so that it has time to settle.

For pre-cooked lasagne sheets, boil them the day before cooking them for the required time which is usually about 20 minutes. Then, put the saucepan in the sink and allow cold water to run through the cooked pasta, slowly. When it's cold and you are able to place your hands in the water, place the sheets in a tray, one on top of each other. Pour cold water onto the tray and fill to the top, as they need to be covered to retain their moisture. Add a little oil in the water.

I usually make the Bolognaise sauce the day before so that it has time to settle.

BECHAMEL SAUCE

INGREDIENTS

- 1 litre milk
- 1 ½ cups flour
- 100g butter
- Pinch of nutmeg
- Salt/pepper to taste

PREPARATION TIME: about 10 minutes

COOKING TIME: about 15 minutes

EQUIPMENT YOU WILL NEED

Medium saucepan - Wooden spoon

METHOD STOVETOP

There are many ways to make Béchamel sauce. This is my way. I place all of the ingredients together and slowly stirring constantly, until it boils and the sauce is thick and smooth.

BOLOGNAISE SAUCE

Carmela's Cucina Povera recipe

INGREDIENTS

- 1kg coarse beef mince
- 1kg coarse pork mince
- 2 x 400 grams cans diced tomatoes
- 250g can tomato paste (after you have added this to the sauce add 1 can of water)
- 2 medium brown onions
- 2 medium carrots (grated)
- ½ a celery (diced)
- Handful of freshly torn basil
- 2 garlic cloves (crushed)
- 4 bay leaves
- Olive oil for browning and cooking
- 1 sprig rosemary
- 1 sprig lemon thyme leaves
- Salt/pepper to taste

PREPARATION TIME: about 20 minutes

COOKING TIME: about 2 hours

EQUIPMENT YOU WILL NEED

Large saucepan - Wooden spoon - Medium chopping board

Medium chopping knife

METHOD STOVETOP

In a large saucepan, with a little oil, brown the onion, carrots and celery until they are golden in colour and not too caramelised. Then, add the beef and pork and allow to cook right through, stirring often.

When the meat is browned, add the tomatoes, tomato paste and garlic. Add a little water and bring the sauce to the boil. Once boiled, put on a low heat and allow to cook for at least 1 ½ to 2 hours. If it gets too thick just add a little water. To test your Bolognese, place your wooden spoon in the sauce. If it feels smooth you are on your way. Then, add the basil and bay leaves and other herbs. I always tie the thyme and rosemary together with kitchen string and remove with the bay leaves when the sauce is ready. Add salt/pepper to taste.

TIP: If you want a great bolognaise, add a whole carrot as it makes the dish very sweet.

PASTA NERA

Nonna Santa, nonna Carmela and my mother Sarina's recipe, updated by Carmela

SERVES 2

INGREDIENTS

- 2 whole calamari
- 1 red onion (diced)
- 400g tin diced tomatoes
- 400g tin of water (use above for measurement)
- 4 tablespoons tomato paste
- Freshly chopped basil leaves
- ½ fresh chilli
- 2 garlic cloves (crushed)
- Sack of ink from calamari
- Virgin olive oil
- Salt/pepper to taste

Image on following page.

PREPARATION TIME: about 20 minutes

COOKING TIME: about 1 hour

EQUIPMENT YOU WILL NEED

Frying pan - Medium chopping board

Medium chopping knife - Large saucepan

METHOD STOVETOP

Clean the calamari, removing the ink from the body keeping the ink sack intact as you will need it later. You can ask your local fish shop to clean the calamari for you.

Slice the calamari into small rings and place them together with the red onions into the frying pan, allowing them to sweat out the residue of their own water on a low her. Stir continuously with a wooden spoon until the water has evaporated. Next, add the diced tomatoes, water, tomato paste and chilli, stir bringing to the boil, then simmer.

Pierce the ink sack of the calamari with a fork and allow the black ink, to drop into the sauce. Stir the sauce and add the virgin olive oil, salt/pepper, garlic, allowing it to simmer for about an hour, stirring occasionally.

About half an hour before the sauce is ready, add freshly chopped basil and serve with your favourite pasta. The pasta soaks up the flavours. Pappardelle and spaghetti are both ideal for this dish. My grandmother liked to use vermicelli. Then we would grate baked ricotta on top of the sauce.

You could hear a pin drop when we ate this dish!

There is a golden rule that my family follows when we eat this dish – silenzio e d'oro.

We would only talk after we ate with mouths full of black ink and laugh at each other! To this day we still do it. Every time I eat it, I think of family members who have passed on with great love and admiration for the foundations of my culture and my values.

Pasta Nera:
   You could hear a pin drop when we ate this dish! There is a golden rule that my family follows when we eat this dish - silenzio e d'oro.

Each region has its own version of this sauce. It's often made with cuttlefish, but I am not a fan. I prefer to use calamari in this dish and I've been doing it for decades.

TOMATO SAUCE DAY

I would love to be able to replay the video that plays in my mind every year as a child growing up and making tomato sauce for the year.

My nonno would save all the tomatoes that he had grown for the month and we would then have a day on which we would cook the sauce in a big barrel with a fire underneath and bottle it the next day, That was our sauce for the year. Every local Sicilian family member would perform this ritual and they would swear that theirs was the best.

Full of pride, they would trade it with each other. We would gather together all day and laugh and yell and tell each other off.

When my grandparents passed away, my father continued this tradition with my mother. Some of us still make our own tomato sauce on a special day. Tomato Sauce Day was a day of reuniting the family and making it together.

ESSENTIAL SECRET INGREDIENTS

Family, fun, laughter, an Italian apron and an Italian song, Mina Tintarella di Luna

NAPOLI SAUCE

Nonno Jack, nonna Carmela and my mother Sarina's recipe, updated by Carmela

This was the first sauce I ever made with my nonno, Giovacchino (Jack) Amato. Every time I make this meal he is with me in spirit. I can remember where I was and when I made it with him. I remember his face and what he was wearing. It was my very first Cucina Povera 'master class' with the master himself. It was such a privilege!

There are several ways to make a traditional Napolitana sauce. I would like to share a version with you that is fast and easy to make, yet bursting with flavour.

I am giving you a great base to work with. Play around with it! You can add protein like diced chicken or vegetables. Add pasta and you have a balanced diet.

Why not make a batch to keep in your fridge and reheat when you are too busy? You can reheat it in a wok on a high heat when you have added all your ingredients. Why have takeaway when you can easily cook this dish?

With this dish, I recommend using grated Parmesan cheese or Pecorino. My favourite addition is Romano, made my Millel. True Sicilians use baked ricotta, grated and it is to die for! You have to try it!

SERVES 2

INGREDIENTS

- 400g tin diced tomatoes
- 1 garlic clove (crushed)
- Freshly torn basil leaves
- Virgin olive oil
- Sea Salt/pepper to taste

PREPARATION TIME: about 15 minutes

COOKING TIME: about 20 minutes

EQUIPMENT YOU WILL NEED

Sauté pan

Medium chopping knife

Medium chopping board

Wooden spoon

METHOD STOVETOP

Place the diced tomatoes in a sauté pan on a high heat and cook to allow the juices to evaporate. This will take about 10 to 15 minutes. Next, drizzle the tomatoes with virgin olive oil, adding the garlic, basil and sea salt/pepper. Cook on low for about 5 minutes and serve with your favourite pasta.

PASTA ALLA NORMA

Carmela's Cucina Povera recipe

Pasta alla norma is a classic pasta dish in Sicilian cuisine from Catania, an Italian city on the east coast of Sicily. It's made with tomatoes, fried aubergine (eggplants), grated ricotta salata cheese and basil. It is supposedly named for the opera Norma by Vincenzo Bellini.

SERVES 2

INGREDIENTS

- Handful of baby rocket leaves
- Baked ricotta for grating
- 400g tin diced tomatoes
- ½ a tin of water to add to sauce
- 1 whole eggplant (diced)
- 1 garlic clove (crushed)
- Freshly torn basil leaves
- Virgin olive oil
- Sea Salt/pepper to taste

PREPARATION TIME: about 20 minutes

COOKING TIME: about 20 minutes

EQUIPMENT YOU WILL NEED

Medium frying pan - Medium chopping board

Medium chopping knife - Strainer - Wooden spoon

METHOD STOVETOP

TIP: Half an hour before you fry the eggplants, dice them and place on a baking tray. Sprinkle with sea salt and leave on the kitchen bench. This allows them to sweat and when you fry them they will not consume as much oil.

Place the eggplants in the frying pan and cook until they are a medium brown. Then add the diced tomatoes and cook on a medium heat. If you are in a hurry, cook on a high heat stirring constantly with a wooden spoon.

Allow the water from the tomatoes to reduce until the sauce appears a little dry which will take about 10-15 minutes. When it has reduced, place it to one side and add garlic, basil, seasoning and virgin olive oil. Return to the heat and cook on a low heat for about 5 minutes.

Your sauce will have a velvety look, like the Italian flag.

Next, add your favourite pasta. Penne is strongly associated with this dish. Grate baked ricotta on top of this sauce and it is absolutely delicious.

TIP: If you want amazing flavour, always add fresh basil about 5 minutes before the sauce is finished cooking, as basil loses its flavour while cooking.

Strain your pasta and gently add the Napoli sauce and stir it in. If the pasta is sticky, add extra virgin olive oil. Don't be afraid ... you are in control! Taste it and see what it needs. You might want to add more seasoning. Close your eyes and connect with your senses.

ADDING EXTRA INGREDIENTS IN NAPOLI SAUCE

You can add proteins to this sauce like tuna, diced cooked chicken (left over from roasts), spinach or even rocket. You can even add fresh ricotta. Want something more health conscious? Add cottage cheese instead.

MAKING A RICHER SAUCE

If you have a few extra people and you want your sauce to be more full-bodied, simply add a bottle of the Passata, can be found in the supermarket shelves. There are many on the shelves to choose from. I prefer Divella sauce. It will just be as tasty. You will need to cook it at a low heat for about 50 minutes to an hour until the water has reduced.

CARCIOFI RIPIENI

My mother Sarina and zia Tonia's recipe, updated by Carmela

This recipe has been changed and modified. Within it are memories of my mother Sarina and my auntie Tonia and myself. The cooking techniques in this recipe come from several generations of women from both sides of my family. Their cooking techniques are amazing.

My auntie zia Tonia Amato cooked meals for me as a young girl and she had her own restaurant with my zio Nino my father's brother, called Albury Pizza Restaurant, in Dean Street, Albury. She did not need qualifications, as she cooked and still cooks with her senses, from her soul and her heritage. I can't tell you how she makes flavours burst in your mouth. She is another pillar in my life and is an amazing woman.

Whenever I visit any of my mother's sisters zia (aunts) Anna Ragusa or my zia Nina Triolo, the first thing they ask me 'is have I eaten'. Even if I already have, I will still eat again. This is a ritual that continues even in the present day.

Anna and Nina are the only elders left from my mother's side of the family here in Australia and my zia Pina, who lives in Sicily. When I visit them I always feel the strong and courageous presence of my late mother Sarina. When she passed away in 2014, she handed onto me the extra bonuses of courage and strength, as she knew that I would need it to continue my journey on this earth.

> Essential secret ingredients:
> Having an auntie or uncle you love, plenty of laughter and smiles all around and plenty of conversation.

CARCIOFI RIPIENI

My mother Sarina and zia Tonia's recipe, updated by Carmela

SERVES 4

INGREDIENTS

- 4 large artichokes (in season)
- 1 ½ cups stale bread (soaked in milk and drained)
- 3 eggs
- Romano cheese
- Parsley (diced)
- Peas 2 cups
- 250g beef mince
- ½ cup rice
- Red onion (diced)
- Virgin olive oil
- 2 litres water or vegetable stock
- Flour for sealing
- Salt/pepper to taste

PREPARATION TIME: about 20 minutes

COOKING TIME: about 90 minutes

EQUIPMENT YOU WILL NEED

Large saucepan with lid - Wooden spoon - Chopping board - Chopping knife

METHOD STOVETOP

Rinse the artichokes. Open them gently so that you can fill them up with the mixture. Allow them to drain on a tea towel upside down.

Meanwhile, add a little virgin olive oil and the red onion to a saucepan and put on a low heat. Let it sweat. Add the peas, followed by stock or water to fill half of the saucepan. Let the liquid boil then simmer slowly.

Next, prepare the mixture for the artichokes; breadcrumbs, Parmesan cheese, rice, mince, parsley, 2 beaten eggs and mix with your hands. Then, open up the artichokes and place about a quarter of a handful of the mixture into the leaves and continue to do this until you have done about 2 layers, if you can.

When you have finished, beat an egg and dip the top of the artichoke into the egg and seal with flour. Then fry the top of the artichokes on medium heat as it helps to further seal them. Then place the artichokes standing upright into the stew made with peas and let it cook slowly with the lid half on, for about one and a half hours.

This is a very satisfying dish that is a nutritious, satisfying meal in itself.

FUN WITH FRITTATA

A frittata is an egg-based dish similar to an omelette. The word frittata, comes from the Italian word friggere, which translated literally means fried. It is enriched by adding ingredients such as vegetables, protein or pasta. I even add leftover cooked rice.

When you are cooking a frittata, your eggs need to be vigorously beaten, to incorporate air, to allow a fuller filling and a fluffier result. The mixture needs to be cooked on a low heat first and then placed in the oven to reach its full colour.

FRITTATA WITH FAVI BEANS AND ARTICHOKES

Carmela's Cucina Povera recipe

SERVES 2

INGREDIENTS

- 4 small artichokes when in season
- 1 cup Favi beans (broad beans) cleaned and skin removed
- ½ cup spring onions
- 1 cup Romano cheese (grated)
- 6 eggs (whisked)
- ¼ cup parsley
- 1 garlic clove (crushed)
- Sea salt/ pepper to taste

PREPARATION TIME: about 20 minutes

COOKING TIME: about 15 minutes

EQUIPMENT YOU WILL NEED

Medium frying pan

medium chopping board

medium chopping knife

Egg flipper

METHOD STOVETOP

Clean and cut the artichokes into slices. I usually just boil the artichokes and broad beans for about 5 minutes to make them edible.

Next, drain them and start preparing the other ingredients. Pan fry the spring onions, artichokes and Favi beans, until they are golden brown and cooked which takes about 4 minutes. Meanwhile, whisk the eggs in a separate bowl.

Then add them to the pan, with the parsley, garlic, Romano cheese, salt/pepper and let the frittata cook until it gets puffy. Make a cross in the pan and turn the frittata over. It will take about a further 3 to 4 minutes to cook. Serve on a plate with a salad or vegetables.

ESSENTIAL SECRET INGREDIENTS

Taking time out to see a friend and making the frittatas with them. Have a glass of wine and enjoy good conversation.

FRITTATA CON PISELLI

Carmela's Cucina Povera recipe

SERVES 2

INGREDIENTS

- 1 small sweet potato (diced and peeled)
- 1 cup peas
- ¼ pumpkin (diced and peeled)
- ½ cup spring onions (finely chopped)
- 8 eggs (whisked)
- 2 cups Romano cheese (grated)
- ½ cup parsley (diced)
- sea salt/pepper

PREPARATION TIME: about 20 minutes

COOKING TIME: about 20 minutes

Preheat a 180°C oven for 20 minutes

EQUIPMENT YOU WILL NEED

Cast iron frying pan

Chopping board

Chopping knife

Egg whisk

Ceramic bowl

Saucepan

Egg flipper

METHOD STOVETOP/OVEN

Boil the sweet potato, peas and pumpkin for about 15 minutes and drain. You need to use a cast iron frying pan that you can put in the oven. Meanwhile, whisk the eggs in a bowl. (Refer to my tip on page 134 about eggs.)

Cook the spring onions then add the eggs to the frypan along with the cooked vegetables. Top with cheese, parsley and season with sea salt and cracked pepper. Allow to cook on a medium heat for about 6 to 10 minutes. The sides of the frittata will start to puff up.

Then put in the oven at 180°C and allow to cook for a further 15 to 20 minutes. You will know it is cooked when you put a fork in the middle and the egg is firm.

Place it the on bench, cut and serve with a salad.

PART THREE
FUSION:
DISCOVERING THE OLD, EMBRACING THE NEW

"I've come to believe that each of us has a personal calling that's as unique as a fingerprint – and that the best way to succeed is to discover what you love and then find a way to offer it to others in the form of service, working hard, and also allowing the energy of the universe to lead you."

.... Oprah Winfrey

ACCEPTANCE

Today is one of the best times in the world to be living in a multicultural society. There is a strong acceptance of multiculturalism.

The United States we now have an African-American president. It wasn't that long ago that some members of society wouldn't have accepted that. Slowly, the world has been showing us that acceptance of each other's culture is the way to achieve freedom from the mind and freedom from old ways of thinking.

Our children's minds are broader than their elders and slowly, our children and the generations to come, can help us shift towards more accepting mindsets.

As a woman with a multicultural background, I have come to a realisation that everyone has the freedom to be who they are. Over the decades, I have learned that we are all equal. I have learned that no person is better than the other and that we all have the best of our culture to offer to the world.

If I give you my best, that will give you the freedom for you to give me your best.

Sharing my culture with you through my journey towards self-acceptance, is total freedom. Accepting who I am and having a strong sense of who I am, enables me to communicate openly and easily with you, with my elders and with my children, giving everyone that I come in contact with, the strength and assurance to believe in themselves.

I believe there is no greater gift for me to give to another person, or to my children and grandchildren, than the gifts of acceptance, communication, love and hope.

I have also accepted that elements of my culture are disappearing, making way for the new. I am proud of sharing the best of my culture with the next generation who can take elements from my culture as they wish.

PESTO

Pesto was often made in the summertime when there was an abundance of fresh basil grown in the vegetable gardens. I am not sure who created it, but I am sure many nonnas tried to utilise whatever ingredients they had to preserve it for the rest of the year.

I make up my own pesto throughout the year.

PESTO ALLA

Cucina Povera – Carmela's Way

This is a very popular dish that is known around the world – it is just a simple meal and not many people know that it is from Cucina Povera.

I have added a few ingredients to this dish. Because I have made it so many times with my husband Marco, we've added ingredients that we love and have experimented with. It is the basic Cucina Povera pesto dish that is one of my husband's all-time favourites.

This dish is a perfect representation of fusion. We've merged ingredients from the past with the present to make a dish that's ready for the future. This dish is like me – a blend of many different eras, different times and experiences. And yet it's also unique and authentic!

Essential secret ingredients:

Be happy, stop and smell the rosemary (that's a saying I have). Enjoy cooking and do it with a smile. Hug the one you love

PESTO ALLA CUCINA POVERA

Carmela's recipe

SERVES: 2

INGREDIENTS
- 2 cups cream
- 1 cup pesto
- 1 cup ricotta
- 8 butterflied king prawns
- 2 tablespoons virgin olive oil
- ½ cup of grated parmesan cheese
- Salt/pepper to taste
- Pre-cooked pasta

PREPARATION TIME: about 5 minutes

COOKING TIME: about 30 minutes

EQUIPMENT YOU WILL NEED

Aldi large frying pan - Wooden spoon - Paring knife

METHOD STOVETOP

Place the oil in a frying pan on a low heat and add the king prawns. When they are cooked, you can see that they turn a red/orange colour. Add the cream, pesto, and ricotta, stirring until the mixture gets a medium to thick consistency.

Take the frying pan off the heat and add your favourite pre-cooked pasta to the sauce. Usually it would be spaghetti, penne/rigatoni or pappardelle. It just depends on what you desire.

TIP: To butterfly the king prawns, start where the body starts. Use a paring knife and cut diagonally into the back of the prawn. You don't slice it completely - you just butterfly it. It opens up when you cook it. It looks lovely and it also cooks quicker.

· ·

PESTO

Carmela's Cucina Povera recipe

INGREDIENTS
- 3 bunches of basil
- 2 bunches of flat parsley
- 3 cloves of garlic
- ½ cup walnuts
- ½ cup virgin olive oil

PREPARATION TIME: about 15 minutes

EQUIPMENT YOU WILL NEED

Food processor, blender or Bamix

METHOD BENCHTOP

Make sure that the basil and parsley are washed and the stalks removed. Tea towel dry the herbs before you put them into your food processor or blender with the other ingredients and blend until smooth. This pesto keeps in the fridge for weeks. Store in a clean jar – you can preserve it by topping with oil. When it gets dry it might get mould on top, but the inside always stays fresh, so just scoop the mould away and discard.

SALADS

Summer is so much fun! It's a great time for salads. Here is a delicious summer dish that I prepare for my husband Marco. I've merged a basic Cucina Povera salad with a dish I've created by experimenting in my kitchen and by being a willing pupil wanting to learn and create.

With all the different seasonal produce you can create great dishes and eat delicious green vegetables and tomatoes that are in season. Fresh basil is plentiful, as well as local red onions and fresh beans. Summer is an amazing time for refreshing your mindset and looking at life in a different way, you get to relax and eat healthily and enjoy the sun. Spend more time with your family and mostly enjoy life.

ESSENTIAL SECRET INGREDIENTS

Sitting in the sunshine while eating. Have a glass of Prosecco. Listening to the birds and looking up at the sky and taking deep breaths

INSALATA DI PESCI (FISH SALAD)

Carmela's Cucina Povera recipe

SERVES: 2

INGREDIENTS

- 2 Basa fillets or tuna steaks (you need a fish that's soft yet firm and holds its texture)
- ½ cup red onion (sliced)
- 2 cups truss tomatoes/cherry tomatoes (diced)
- 2 cups cucumbers (diced)
- 1 lemon, freshly squeezed
- Virgin olive oil
- ½ an iceberg lettuce, broken into chunks
- 1 cup rocket
- 1 avocado (I usually break it up with a spoon and take it out spoon by spoon. That way it retains its consistency and doesn't go brown)
- 1 cup parsley (chopped)
- 2 basil leaves (chopped)
- Canola oil
- Salt/pepper to taste

PREPARATION TIME: about 15 minutes

COOKING TIME: about 30 minutes

EQUIPMENT YOU WILL NEED

Large chopping board

Paring knife

Large chopping knife

Chargrill plate/frying pan

METHOD STOVETOP

Place the fish onto a chargrill plate or frying pan and cook for about 10 minutes, constantly turning and adding a small amount of canola oil, as it helps to stop the fish from sticking to the plate. Then place the fish onto a plate. Next, put all the other ingredients into a mixing bowl and mix with your hands. Then add the cooked fish. This meal is full of amazing flavours that burst in your mouth and is a well-balanced dish.

TIP: As a variation, you can add king prawns or sliced poached chicken. I even add fried calamari.

INSALATA DI MARCO CON AMORE

Carmela's Cucina Povera recipe

SERVES: 1

INGREDIENTS
- ½ an iceberg lettuce
- 1 avocado
- ½ red onion (chopped into strips)
- Juice of ½ a lemon
- 2 tablespoons virgin olive oil

I also make this salad for my husband Marco, as he loves salad with a lot of flavour. He is a diabetic and doesn't like vinegar, so I add a lot of lemon juice (which is great for his condition).

PREPARATION TIME: about 10 minutes

EQUIPMENT YOU WILL NEED

Medium chopping board

Paring knife

Salad bowl

METHOD BENCHTOP

Wash the iceberg lettuce and shake out the excess water. Break into small pieces and place into a bowl.

Cut the red onion into strips and spoon the avocado into the salad. Next, add virgin olive oil, lemon juice, salt/pepper to taste and toss. This is a base for many of my salads and I add many other ingredients to this basic salad to create a meal.

TIP: You can add 2 boiled eggs to this salad. Usually, I place the boiled eggs into my palm and using a fork in the other hand, grate it into the mixture.

I also add a poached chicken breast, sliced very thinly. It's very nutritious and quick, especially if you have pre-prepared all of the other ingredients.

CAPRESE INSALATA

SERVES: 2

INGREDIENTS

- 2 tomatoes (truss tomatoes or 1 punnet of cherry tomatoes)
- 3 Buffalo Mozzarella bocconcini
- 4 basil leaves (sliced)
- Virgin olive oil
- Pesto
- Salt/pepper to taste

This is a timeless salad. I love playing around with this dish. Insalata Caprese means Salad of Capri. It is a simple Italian salad, made of sliced fresh Mozzarella, tomatoes and basil, seasoned with salt and virgin olive oil. It was made to resemble the colours of the Italian flag: red, white and green. In Italy, it was usually served as an antipasto (starter). The island of Capri is situated just outside of Sorrento, Italy, near Naples.

PREPARATION TIME: about 10 minutes

EQUIPMENT YOU WILL NEED

Chopping board - Paring knife

METHOD BENCHTOP

Wash and slice the tomatoes and place onto a serving plate. Break the buffalo Mozzarella into small pieces and place on top of the tomatoes. Using a small spoon gently place the pesto on top of the buffalo Mozzarella, followed by the basil, olive oil and salt/pepper. With this timeless salad, you can add rocket and fresh anchovies and you have a beautiful blend of fresh ingredients. If you don't have fresh basil, add additional pesto on top.

DI FAGIOLI E POMODORI (BEAN AND TOMATO SALAD)

Carmela's Cucina Povera recipe

INGREDIENTS

- 300g jar of butter or haricot beans (rinsed and drained)
- 2 tomatoes (de-seeded) and cut in strips
- ½ bunch basil leaves (torn)
- 1 red onion (sliced into half moon shapes)
- 1 tablespoon red wine vinegar
- 2 tablespoons extra virgin olive oil
- Salt/pepper to taste

SERVES: 2

PREPARATION TIME: about 15 minutes

EQUIPMENT YOU WILL NEED

Medium chopping board - Paring knife - Can opener

Salad plate for serving

METHOD KITCHEN BENCH

Place the beans, tomatoes, basil and onion into a bowl. Mix well. Whisk oil, vinegar, salt and pepper to make a dressing and toss it carefully through the salad.

INSALATA DI PATATI (POTATO SALAD)

My mother Sarina's recipe

SERVES: 4–6

INGREDIENTS

- 10 baby chat potatoes
- 1 red onion
- ½ kg fresh green beans
- A sprinkle of fresh oregano
- Virgin olive oil
- 1 clove garlic (crushed)
- Salt/pepper to taste

My mother taught me to make this dish. She added boiled eggs instead of beans. We used to eat this regularly in the summer when we were having BBQs and all she had were potatoes from the vegetable garden and red onions.

PREPARATION TIME: about 20 minutes

EQUIPMENT YOU WILL NEED

Medium chopping board

Large saucepan

Paring knife

Salad bowl

METHOD STOVETOP

Boil the potatoes for about 20 minutes. Drain and allow to cool, leaving the lid on the saucepan. This lets them sweat which will make the skins easier to peel.

In another saucepan, boil the fresh green beans, allowing them to cook for about 20 minutes.

Next, finely slice the red onion and add to a large salad bowl – ideally one that is wide and not too deep, which makes it easier to toss the salad.

Peel the potatoes and cut them in half. Place them in the bowl, with the beans and red onion.

Sprinkle with a little oregano, salt/pepper, a drizzle of virgin olive oil and the garlic and toss. And there you have a beautiful salad, for any summer barbeque that complements any meat dish.

INSALATA DI PEPERONI ROSTITI (GRILLED ROASTED RED PEPPERS)

My mother Sarina's recipe

SERVES: 3

INGREDIENTS
- 6 red peppers
- Oregano
- Virgin olive oil
- 1 clove of crushed garlic

PREPARATION TIME: about 30 minutes

COOKING TIME: about 50 minutes

Preheat a 200°C oven for 20 minutes

EQUIPMENT YOU WILL NEED

Plastic bag for sweating peppers

Serving plate

Oven tray for baking

METHOD OVEN/BBQ

Wash and wipe down the red capsicums with a paper towel and place them on the baking tray and then into an oven preheated to 200°C. Cook until the skin comes away from the meat of the peppers - you need to turn them over a few times so they cook evenly. It will look as though they are being burnt.

Next, place them into a plastic bag for about half an hour. The bag makes them sweat and the skin will be easier to peel. Remove the skins and place the capsicums onto a large serving plate. Tear up the capsicum meat and add the olive oil, garlic, oregano and garlic and toss together. Your dish is now ready to serve.

This side dish tastes amazing when you cook it on a barbeque, as the flavours become infused. I.usually eat this nutritious dish with a veal cottoletta or with fennel sausages, another side salad and crusty bread
(like ciabatta).

FISH

Sicilians love seafood and it is a major part of the Sicilian diet.

I know that eating fish has always been a bigger part of our diet than meat, mainly because we come from the coast of Sicily. Fish was the main protein we ate, because our fathers and grandfathers were fishermen.

My mother Sarina used to tell me that a few times a year people would come to see my grandfather Stefano and they would bring either a pig or a goat and he would give them preserved tuna that he had in storage. My grandfather had a room where he kept preserved tuna all year round.

Fish is really healthy and there are a lot of ways to prepare it. My mother Sarina used to make polpetti di pesce (fish meatballs) out of several different kinds of fish. She would use whiting fillets, garfish fillets, salmon fillets and tuna fillets. For me it is easy to cook with fish as it so versatile.

The flavours are enhanced when you add Parmesan cheese, fresh parsley, crushed garlic and homemade breadcrumbs. Mum would also cook fish in her famous Napoli sauce that she bottled from the summer season and kept for the year. She would cook the sauce for hours and add cooked pasta. So we used to eat pasta with the sauce and have the fish meatballs as a second meal.

There are so many different types of fish that you can eat. My favourites are tuna, swordfish, baccala, stoccafisso, nunata (our dialect version for little whitebait,) small garfish, whiting and flounder.

In Sicily/Italy, swordfish is a commonly eaten dish, like tuna. The best place to get swordfish is from the belly where you can source the more delicate flavours.

"Our fathers a

PESCE SPADA ALLA MILLAZZESI (SWORDFISH, MILLAZZO-STYLE)

My mother Sarina's recipe, updated by Carmela

SERVES: 4

INGREDIENTS

- 10 green olives in brine
- Extra virgin olive oil
- 4 x 140g fresh swordfish steaks
- Sea salt and freshly ground black pepper
- 2 spring onions (chopped)
- 2 garlic cloves (chopped)
- 20g salted capers, rinsed and well drained
- A pinch of dried chilli flakes
- 4 anchovy fillets in oil
- 70ml white wine
- 1 x 400g tin of chopped tomatoes
- 1 tablespoon parsley
- A sprig of lemon thyme

PREPARATION TIME: about 15 minutes

COOKING TIME: about 50 minutes

Preheat a 200°C oven for 20 minutes

EQUIPMENT YOU WILL NEED

Large frying pan with lid or casserole dish

Large chopping board

Large chopping knife

Wooden spoon

METHOD STOVETOP

Drain the olives and pat them dry. Halve them and remove the pips. Heat some extra virgin olive oil in a casserole dish and add the swordfish. Season and seal the fish on both sides then place on a side dish.

Next, add the spring onions, garlic, capers, olives, chilli and anchovy fillets and cook gently until the anchovies melt into the oil and the onion becomes translucent. Then, add the white wine. Allow the liquid to bubble (to evaporate the alcohol). Then add the tomatoes mixing well.

Cover and leave to cook for about 30 minutes on a very low heat, adding the swordfish as well as the lemon thyme for the last 10 to 12 minutes. Serve sprinkled with parsley and a drizzle of virgin olive oil.

ESSENTIAL SECRET INGREDIENTS
A red and white checked tablecloth
Sitting with your family at the table
Plenty of conversation

BACCALA-STOCCAFISSO STUFATO (SALTED COD AND STOCK FISH STEW)

Baccala is one of the most commonly eaten types of fish across Sicily. I have eaten this dish throughout my life. My mother would make this at Christmastime and on other special occasions. When I visited Sicily it was a dish I made all the time as it brought back memories of my childhood. When I eat this dish, I remember my grandfather Jack and my mother Sarina. Meals bring back many memories! I still can't make this dish as well as my mother could, regardless of how much I try!

. . . .

BACCALA AND STOCCAFISSO

I'm told that the difference between the two is in the curing process and not in the type of fish.

Baccala is a cod that has been salted on the ship and dried on land. It consists of large chunks or a side of fish and it is only light dried. Prior to use it may need to be soaked in water for at least 24 hours. It is also sold already prepared for cooking, across Sicily/Italy.

Every region has its own way of preparing it. In Liguria/Italy, it is cooked with spinach (baccala in zimino*) or fried and served with a sauce made from fresh breadcrumbs and chopped garlic.

In Tuscany, baccala alla fiorentina is pan-fried and stewed in tomato sauce, while in Rome the baccala is coated in a light batter to which whipped egg white has been added and then deep fried.

A recipe from Abruzzo combines baccala with celery, pine nuts, sultanas, black olives and tomatoes. A similar dish is made in Naples, while another Neapolitan recipe adds grilled peppers to the fried fish.

In Sicily most fish is served on Fridays. This is because Sicilians are very religious and Fridays are commonly meat-free.

Nowadays, baccala is cooked far less at home because it's expensive to buy, but it still appears in the local trattorias. When my parents prepared the pesce stocco, they would cut it into small pieces and soak it in water for about five to seven days changing the water daily. It is a very stinky fish and my suggestion would be to put it in your laundry!

*In Zimino is a Tuscan term that means cooked with greens.

STOCCAFISSO STUFATO (STEWED STOCK FISH)

My mother Sarina's recipe, updated by Carmela

SERVES: 4

INGREDIENTS

- 1 whole stoccafisso pre-cut and presoaked
- 400g tin diced tomatoes
- Half a tin of water
- 1 large onion (diced)
- 1 cup Sicilian olives with pips
- 3 large potatoes (quartered)
- Virgin olive oil
- 1 clove garlic (crushed)
- 1 handful parsley (diced)
- ½ red chilli (diced)

PREPARATION TIME: about 20 minutes

COOKING TIME: about 2 hours

EQUIPMENT YOU WILL NEED

Casserole dish or sauté frying pan with lid

Large chopping board

Large chopping knife

Paring knife

Vegetable peeler

The presoaking process for stoccafisso in cold water lasts for about six days, changing the water daily. Today you can buy it ready-made from your local Italian grocer. You still have to soak it the day before you eat it in cold water as it has been preserved with salt.

METHOD STOVETOP

Brown the onion with some oil in a casserole dish, adding the diced tomatoes and water. Allow to boil then simmer. Then add the stoccafisso, the potatoes, olives, crushed garlic and chilli, allowing it to cook for about two hours on a low heat, stirring occasionally. Add more water if necessary. When the fish is ready, handle it carefully as it can break very easily. Add fresh parsley.

My grandfather, Giovacchino Amato, would put the baccala into a big saucepan with potatoes and allow it to boil. When the fish was ready, he would remove some of the juice and drain it, adding lemon juice, fresh parsley and virgin olive oil and salt/pepper. He would serve it like a salad.

BACCALA FRITTI (FRIED, SALTED COD)

My nonno Jack's recipe, updated by Carmela

SERVES: 2

INGREDIENTS

- 1/2kg fresh baccala (salted cod) soaked in fresh water the day before cooking
- Handful of parsley (chopped)
- Olive oil
- Fresh lemon

BATTER OPTION - 1

- 250g flour
- 100g cornflour
- A squirt of lemon juice
- Sea salt and cracked pepper
- San Pellegrino sparkling water
- Lemon thyme
- Rosemary/sage (finely chopped)

BATTER OPTION - 2

- 250g plain flour
- 2 eggs
- Lemon thyme/rosemary/sage (finely chopped)
- Sea salt/ pepper to taste
- San Pellegrino sparkling water

PREPARATION TIME: about 15 minutes

COOKING TIME: about 20 minutes

EQUIPMENT YOU WILL NEED

Deep frying pan - Chopping board - Chopping knife

FOR THE BATTER

Ceramic bowl - Wooden spoon - Whisk - Fork

METHOD STOVETOP

Cut the rinsed and drained baccala into small tubes and place it onto kitchen paper. Prepare the batter, mixing the flour, cornflour, salt/pepper and lemon juice. Sprinkle the herbs into the batter and with a fork, mix in the San Pellegrino mineral water until the batter becomes smooth. Dip the baccala into the batter then deep-fry in a large pan with olive oil. When the baccala is golden brown, place it onto a plate with kitchen paper to remove the excess oil. Serve with fresh lemon.

Whisk all of the ingredients together to make a batter.

CALAMARI FRITTI

My mother Sarina's recipe, updated by Carmela

SERVES: 2

INGREDIENTS

- 1kg fresh calamari, cleaned and chopped by the fishmonger
- 2 cups flour
- 1 cup Parmesan cheese (grated)
- 1 cup Panko breadcrumbs
- ½ cup parsley (chopped)
- Vegetable oil for frying
- Sea salt/cracked pepper
- Fresh Lemon

PREPARATION TIME: about 15 minutes

COOKING TIME: about 20 minutes

EQUIPMENT YOU WILL NEED

Deep frying pan - Kitchen paper or greaseproof paper

Chopping knife - Chopping board

METHOD STOVETOP

Place all the ingredients except the calamari into a deep bowl and mix well. Next, add the calamari and coat with the mixture. Just before you fry them you need to sift them in a colander. Heat the vegetable oil in a frypan and place the calamari into the oil. When they are golden brown, remove with a slotted spoon and place onto kitchen paper. Sprinkle with sea salt and cracked pepper and serve with fresh lemon.

CALAMARI SICILIANI RIPIENI (STUFFED CALAMARI SICILIAN STYLE)

My mother Sarina's recipe, updated by Carmela

SERVES: 4

INGREDIENTS

- 4 large calamari, cleaned and tentacles chopped into small cubes by the fishmonger
- 100g Panko breadcrumbs
- 3 cups pre-cooked rice
- ½ handful of Pecorino cheese (grated)
- ½ cup parsley (diced)
- 1 cup baby shrimps
- ½ cup cooked peas
- ½ cup diced flat continental parsley
- ½ cup diced tomatoes
- Napoli sauce for cooking (see page 127 for recipe)
- Olive oil for frying
- Sea salt/cracked pepper

PREPARATION TIME: about 30 minutes

COOKING TIME: about 2 hours

Preheat a 200°C oven for 20 minutes

EQUIPMENT YOU WILL NEED

Ovenproof casserole dish

Chopping board

Paring knife

METHOD STOVETOP/OVEN

Sauté the tentacles and allow them to cool. Make the "filling by combining the baby shrimps, fried tentacles, diced tomatoes, peas, Pecorino, breadcrumbs, parsley, rice, sea salt and cracked pepper. Mix well and stuff into the body of the calamari. Seal the openings with a toothpick and place the stuffed calamari onto a tray.

Next, fry the calamari in a little olive oil, then add the sauce and place into a preheated oven for about an hour and a half at 180°C. You might need to add some fish stock or water to moisten the calamari. When you can put your fork into the calamari and it is soft, you know they're ready.

When I am about to serve the dish I usually pour the Napoli on top of the calamari, drizzle with virgin olive oil, fresh parsley and sprinkle a little grated Pecorino and serve.

Stuffed calamari sicilian style.

PESCI SPADA (SWORDFISH)

Swordfish travel in an anticlockwise direction along the northern coasts of Africa to Asia Minor and back along the coast of Sicily. Once sighted, they are harpooned just as they were in ancient Greek and Roman times.

My maternal grandfather Stefano Salmeri was a Pesci Spadi expert and had his own fishing boat. He raised eight children during a time of war and famine, but with his expertise as a fisherman they didn't go hungry.

Stefano's father, Thomaso Salmeri was also an expert fisherman. They were known all over Sicily and he is still remembered in my mother's hometown, Milazzo, Provincia Messina Sicilia Italia, a fishing port. Many tourists go there to visit the Aeolion islands like Lipari, Vulcano, Isola and Aeoli. There are many more little islands. Milazzo is one of the most beautiful places in Sicily.

SARDINI RIPIENI ALLA MILAZZESI (FILLED SARDINES ALLA MILLAZZO)

My mother Sarina's recipe, updated by Carmela

SERVES: 3

INGREDIENTS

- 12 filleted sardines
- Stale bread made into breadcrumbs
- Pecorino cheese (grated)
- Handful of parsley (chopped)
- Sea salt and freshly cracked pepper
- Egg wash
- Crushed garlic
- Pre-cooked Napoli sauce (see Sauces, on page 127).

PREPARATION TIME: about 20 minutes

COOKING TIME: about 1 hour

EQUIPMENT YOU WILL NEED

Large chopping board · Large chopping knife
Large frying pan

METHOD STOVETOP

Place the sardines onto a board. Combine the breadcrumbs, Pecorino and parsley with a little garlic, and place on top of each sardine.

Put them into a frying pan and slowly brown them. Add the pre-cooked Napoli sauce to the sauce and allow to cook for about half an hour adding extra water if necessary. The sauce should be velvety.

I usually have enough sauce to add a little spaghetti to this dish. Use about 120g per person or just enough to ensure the flavour of the fish comes through the spaghetti. Then I add fresh Pecorino to the spaghetti and mangia!

A TRUE FISHERMAN'S TALE ABOUT MY FATHER

My father Sam and my nonno Giovacchino were fishermen with their own business in Falcone before they came to Australia. My father used to tell me a story of when he was nearly lost at sea at the age of 17.

His little boat took him miles from the shore. It was dark and he was lost. He was cold and suffered from hypothermia. He thought he would die out there on the fierce ocean, as his little boat was tossed about.

He wondered if he would ever see his parents again. He told me it felt like it was forever and he called out all night to the Madonna of his hometown, La Madonna del Tindari *(See en.wikipedia.org/wiki/Tindari for more)*.

Local legend states that the lagoon was created after a pilgrim who came to see the Madonna refused to pray to the Madonna because she was black. The woman accidentally dropped her baby into the ocean and the Madonna made the land rise to save the baby. The sands of Marinello have taken the shape of the profile of the Madonna.

He swears that the Madonna saved him. Whenever he recounted the story, his eyes would widen. He had the most penetrating green eyes. La Madonna del Tindari was his favourite Madonna and he used to visit the sanctuary every time he went home to Falcone. Tindari is where the Madonna del Tindari's sanctuary is situated – about five minutes drive from my father's home town.

His little boat took him miles from the shore. It was dark and he was lost.

EXAMPLES OF FUSING CUCINA POVERA RECIPES

I picked these particular recipes because they are well known and have been around for decades.

There are so many names for Marinara that people get confused. With Marinara – or Pescatore, or Fruitto del Mare – you can make it in several ways: with an oil base or a cream base. Pescatore is tomato based and so is Fruitto del Mare and it contains all kinds of seafood.

You can add clams, soft crabs shells, yabbies, or Moreton Bay bugs and it is called Fruits of the Sea.

Here is the oil-based marinara dish that serves as a benchmark for any Cucina Povera seafood dish.

UNDERSTANDING SEAFOOD TERMS

But firstly I would like to elaborate about the seafood to help you understand more about the names.

Pescatore means fisherman: one who fishes and the dish is known for its Napoli base.
You can add tomatoes instead, if you don't like Napoli or cherry tomatoes.

Marinara has the same meaning but refers to shore fishing. It is usually a virgin olive oil based-dish. Australians love cream, so it has been adapted for Australia with the addition of cream to the dish.

Fruitto Del Mare means fruits of the sea. Here is where you can get creative. Just think of any kind of shellfish that you like (including lobster) and add to this dish.

ESSENTIAL SECRET INGREDIENTS

Being willing to try something that you haven't before.
Having courage.
Enjoying each bite of your meal .
Sitting at the table and having a glass of Italian wine with your meal.

MATRICIANA

Carmela's Cucina Povera recipe

SERVES: 2

INGREDIENTS

- 2 strips long rind bacon/pancetta and mild salami
- 1 cup of spring onions or red onions
- 1 red capsicum (diced)
- Virgin olive oil
- 1 cup pitted olives
- 4 leaves sliced basil
- ½ tablespoon garlic (chopped)
- ½ tablespoon chilli
- 3 big ladles of cooked Napoli sauce (refer to page 127)
- Pre-cooked pasta

PREPARATION TIME: about 15 minutes

COOKING TIME: about 30 minutes

EQUIPMENT YOU WILL NEED

Frying pan

Medium chopping board

Medium chopping knife

Paring knife

METHOD STOVETOP

Place the bacon or pancetta, salami, spring onions and red capsicum into a frying pan, together with the oil. Allow them to. cook on a medium to high heat for about 4 minutes until brown. Then add the Napoli sauce, olives, basil, chilli and garlic and cook for another 3 minutes.

Add your favourite pasta to this sauce, sprinkle with fresh Parmesan/Romano and serve with a beautiful salad. For me the best salad with this dish is Insalata di Marco.

MARINARA FOR 2

My mother Sarina's recipe, updated by Carmela

SERVES: 2

INGREDIENTS

- 6 king prawns
- 10 mussels
- 2 scallops
- 4 clams
- 1 fresh fish, diced tuna steak or flathead fillets)
- 2 cloves garlic (crushed)
- Virgin olive oil
- ½ cup parsley (chopped)
- Pasta

PREPARATION TIME: about 20 minutes

COOKING TIME: about 30 minutes

EQUIPMENT YOU WILL NEED

Large frying pan with lid - Medium chopping board

Medium chopping knife - Paring knife

METHOD STOVETOP

Place the oil, garlic and half of the parsley into a frying pan. Let the ingredients sizzle for about 2 minutes. Next, add the seafood to the pan and cook on a medium heat with the lid on. You only need to cook this for about 4 minutes and the mussels will sweat and open up.

You will find that the seafood contains a lot of water and becomes like a stew. Don't worry, because when you add the pasta much of the liquid will be soaked up.

Cook the pasta. Many Sicilians use pappardelle, linguini or spaghetti, along with extra parsley and a little added oil. Keep the pasta moist and don't let it become dry. You can even add a little of the water from the pasta that you cooked. Serve the pasta with the sauce poured over.

Remember you don't have to follow my instructions to the letter – experiment a little and go with what feels right!

Follow this process and you have a benchmark for Marinara, Pescatore and Fruitto del Mare.

You can add a little cream when you're cooking, or a little Napoli, or even cherry tomatoes. This dish is so versatile and stands on its own as a meal.

SUGGESTIONS: You can have fresh bread at the table and make a beautiful salad. Do this and you'll have won over your guests or even your partner! It only takes about 20 minutes to cook and you can always use pre-cooked pasta (page 112).

There are many ways to make Carbonara that blend old ways of cooking with the new ways. This is why I included it in the Fusion section of this book.

In the Australian version of Carbonara, bacon has become the substitute for pancetta and cream adds flavour and prevents it from drying out. All these beautiful ingredients weave together old and new ways of cooking.

CARBONARA
Carmela's Cucina Povera fusion version

SERVES: 2

INGREDIENTS

- 2 rashers of bacon (diced)
- ½ cup spring onions
- ½ cup baby spinach
- ½ cup porcini mushrooms*
- 2 tablespoons oil
- 1 dollop of butter
- 1 clove of garlic (diced)
- 2 cups cream
- 2 egg yolks
- ½ cup Parmesan cheese
- 2 tablespoons parsley (chopped)
- Pre-cooked pasta

PREPARATION TIME: about 15 minutes

COOKING TIME: about 30 minutes

EQUIPMENT YOU WILL NEED

Medium chopping board - Medium chopping knife - -Frying pan

METHOD STOVETOP

Place oil, butter, garlic, spring onions, bacon, mushrooms, and baby spinach in a frying pan and allow it to cook for about 4 minutes until the bacon becomes golden brown. Add the cream, a tablespoon of parsley and allow the cream to cook until it gets a tan look.

Then add the cooked pasta (see page 118) to the frying pan and allow the juices to infuse. Add half of the parmesan cheese and stir. When thickened, remove pan from the heat, add the eggs and stir, but do not put back on heat as it will cook the eggs. The eggs make the dish become velvety.

Add salt/pepper to taste. Place the cooked dish onto a serving plate, adding extra Parmesan and sprinkle with fresh parsley.

*Porcini mushrooms are most commonly grown under trees and have a rustic look and texture, as they take on the taste of the tree that they have been cultivated under. They are usually grown wild, picked and preserved. You can get them from your local Italian grocer and they need to be placed in water overnight as they are dry from being preserved. I have included porcini with this recipe as it gives a more rustic flavour to the dish.

You can have one of my salads to go with this dish and you have a great nutritious meal.

SOUPS

Essential secret ingredients:
Make it for someone who needs a smile,
plenty of love, kind words a nonna's touch.

This is a dish that I've always eaten when I'm not feeling the best or when I need a pick-me-up. It's packed with protein and vegetables.

I remember my nonna making it for my brother and me. We would just sit, in silenzio and eat.

My nonno used to say silenzio o d'oro which means silence is golden. My grandparents were just the medicine that I needed. The love and comfort that they shared with me was like water slowly watering a tiny seed and allowing it to grow and thrive with time.

CHICKEN SOUL FOOD SOUP

Nonna Carmela's recipe, updated by Carmela

SERVES: 3–4

INGREDIENTS

- 1 whole organic chicken
- 2 potatoes (peeled)
- 2 carrots (peeled)
- 1 onion (diced)
- ¼ cup tomatoes (diced – fresh or tinned)
- ½ celery (diced)
- 1 cup Risoni pasta, or rice, or baby tortellini, or broken spaghetti
- 10 litres of water
- Fresh parsley
- Parmesan cheese, grated

PREPARATION TIME: about 20 minutes

COOKING TIME: about 2 hours

EQUIPMENT YOU WILL NEED

Large saucepan with lid - Chopping board - Tray - Strainer Chopping knife - Passatutto/blender

METHOD STOVETOP

Place the chicken in a large saucepan. Add the other ingredients bring to the boil then cook on a medium to low heat for about two hours always make sure that there is plenty of water, you can add more water.

When cooked, place the chicken onto a tray and allow to cool. While you're waiting for the chicken to cool, remove the saucepan from the heat and blend the ingredients with a stick blender or food processor. Or, you could do what my nonna used to do and pass the ingredients through a Passatutto machine (which involves passing everything through an Italian tomato press).

Add the vegetables that you have just passed through the Passatutto machine or blended, Once the chicken is cool, peel the meat off and add the chicken to the stock, adding water if needed and stir. You can add more fresh parsley if you like and before you serve it, freshly grated Parmesan cheese on top. You can also add your favourite pasta, or rice, or baby tortellini.

SUPER GREEN FOOD SOUP (ZUPPA VERDI)

Carmela's Cucina Povera recipe

INGREDIENTS

> 250g packet green lentils
> 250g packet green split peas
> 2 stalks of celery (diced)
> 1 zucchini (diced)
> 2 cups broccoli (diced)
> 1/2 a kale (diced)
> 4 leaves of silverbeet (diced)
> 1 potato (diced)
> 1 small onion (diced)
> 4 litres of water

SERVES: 2

PREPARATION TIME: about 20 minutes

COOKING TIME: about 1½ – 2 hours

EQUIPMENT YOU WILL NEED

Large saucepan with lid

Medium chopping board

Medium knife

METHOD STOVETOP

Place all the ingredients into a big pan with about four litres of water. Bring to the boil and allow to cook for about an hour on a medium to high heat.

When the ingredients thicken, cook for about another hour on a low heat, stirring occasionally. You know when it is ready because it becomes thick. You can add stock to loosen it up. It's up to you. Choose the consistency you prefer. I like this soup to be thick.

This soup is jam-packed with amazing, nutritious ingredients. It usually lasts in the fridge for about 6 days. Pack some away in the freezer and reheat when you need a quick meal.

This soup is jam-packed with amazing, nutritious ingredients.

ZUPPA GIALLA E ORANGIO (YELLOW AND ORANGE SOUP)

Carmela's Cucina Povera recipe

INGREDIENTS

- ¼ pumpkin (diced and peeled)
- ¼ sweet potato (diced and peeled)
- 1 potato (diced and peeled)
- 1 small onion (diced)
- 3 stalks celery (diced)
- 2 carrots (diced and peeled)
- 2 fresh ears of corn, left whole but clean
- ½ cup barley

SERVES: 2

PREPARATION TIME: about 15 minutes

COOKING TIME: about 1 hour

EQUIPMENT YOU WILL NEED

Medium chopping board

Medium chopping knife

Large saucepan with lid

METHOD STOVETOP

Place all of the ingredients into a saucepan and bring to the boil. Allow to cook for about an hour on a high heat, stirring occasionally. Then turn down the heat to medium for about another half an hour and keep an eye on it so that it doesn't become too thick. You can add water or stock to change the consistency. Remove the corn from the soup and slice the corn off the cob and stir into the soup.

If you can hold off eating the soup for a day, this will allow the flavours to settle in and to develop. Most soups taste better the following day.

Most soups taste better the following day.

ZUPPA DI FAVE E FINOCCHIO (BROAD BEAN AND FENNEL SOUP)

Carmela's Cucina Povera recipe

INGREDIENTS

- 600g dried broad beans, soaked overnight in cold water
- 1 teaspoon fennel (chopped) or 1 teaspoon dried fennel seeds, soaked in water
- 200g fresh broad beans, skin removed
- Olive oil
- 1 small onion (diced finely)
- 1 medium carrot (diced finely)
- 1 celery stalk (diced finely)
- 1 large potato (diced finely)
- 2 litres water or stock
- Sea salt and freshly ground black pepper
- Extra virgin olive oil for finishing

SERVES: 2

PREPARATION TIME: about 15 minutes

COOKING TIME: about 2 hours

EQUIPMENT YOU WILL NEED

Large saucepan with lid

Food processor

Chopping board

Chopping knife

METHOD STOVETOP

Soak the dried broad beans in cold water overnight, then drain them.

In a saucepan, place the soaked beans and the fresh broad beans with the fennel, onion, celery, potato, carrots and a little olive oil on a low heat and allow the vegetables to sweat. Then, add water or stock (about 2 litres) and bring to the boil. Turn down the heat to a simmer and cook for about two hours.

When the mixture thickens, place it into a food processor and blend until smooth. Serve in a soup bowl with a little virgin olive oil and a sprinkle of cracked pepper. This soup is great throughout winter and it can also be served cold throughout summer.

ZUPPA DI LENTICCHIE SICILIANA (SICILIAN LENTIL SOUP)

Carmela's Cucina Povera recipe

INGREDIENTS

- 250g dried lentils or fresh organic canned lentils
- 50g smoky bacon (diced finely)
- 1 onion (chopped finely)
- ½ a red chilli (diced finely)
- 1 large carrot (diced)
- A few sprigs of fennel (chopped)
- 2 celery stalks (finely chopped)
- Olive oil
- Sea salt and cracked pepper

SERVES: 4

PREPARATION TIME: about 20 minutes

COOKING TIME: about 1 hour

EQUIPMENT YOU WILL NEED

Chopping board - Large saucepan with lid - Chopping knife

METHOD STOVETOP

Slowly fry the bacon in a little olive oil. Next, add the chopped onion, diced carrot, celery and the chilli. When the onion is soft, stir in the beef stock.
Carefully rinse the dried lentils and add them to the pot, along with the fennel, the bouquet of fresh herbs, the tomato concentrate and season. Bring the dish to a gentle simmer and allow to cook for about 30 minutes.
Check to see if you need to add more stock. Bring it to the boil and add ditalini pasta. Cook until the pasta is al dente and serve, adding a drizzle of virgin olive oil.

VEAL RECIPES

Veal is a great way to get your protein without the fat. You can make many dishes with veal and it's fun to experiment with.

Veal has been an important ingredient in Italian cooking from ancient times. It is often in the form of cutlets or Italian cottoletta. It's lower in fat than many other types of meat and care must be taken in preparation to ensure that it does not become tough when you cook it. Veal is often coated in preparation for frying or with sauces. A common Italian American dish is Parmigiana.

Essential secret ingredients: Plenty of good conversation, plenty of questions and family time.

VEAL PARMIGIANA

After you have fried or chargrilled the Veal Cotoletta, add the heated pre-cooked Napoli sauce (see page 127) on top of the veal (like a coating, depending on the texture and consistency that you prefer). Then add some diced basil on top and grated Mozzarella cheese. Place the veal onto a baking tray and place under the grill or in your oven to melt the cheese.

I use a salamander (a culinary broiler) in my restaurant, which makes life easier. Serve the Veal Parmigiana with your favourite sides.

VEAL COTOLETTI (VEAL SCHNITZELS)

My mother Sarina's recipe, updated by Carmela

INGREDIENTS

- 2 x 200g veal schnitzels (uncrumbed)
- 1 egg, beaten with a little milk to soften the mixture and salt/pepper
- 3 cups Panko breadcrumbs
- 1 cup Parmesan cheese (grated)
- ½ cup parsley (chopped)
- Flour for coating
- Salt/pepper to taste

SERVES: 2

PREPARATION TIME: about 15 minutes

COOKING TIME: about 10–15 minutes

EQUIPMENT YOU WILL NEED

Chopping board

Meat tenderiser

Frying pan

Bowls

Flat oven trays

METHOD STOVETOP

Place the veal on a chopping board and beat with a tenderiser. When the veal becomes transparent, place to one side.

Next, place all the coating ingredients into a bowl or onto an oven tray and mix well. Coat your veal in flour, dip in the egg wash and then into the coating mixture. The flour gives the veal a good coating and allows the egg and breadcrumbs to seal well. Then fry the Veal Cotoletta in a little olive oil.

This dish goes well with your favourite salad or vegetables. The beauty of cottoletta is that you can spend half an hour making them and then store them for future use. You may want to make a Parmigiana with it as well.

Cotoletta means coated in Italian. We usually coat chicken, veal, beef and pork. It is derived from the name Weiner Schnitzel. It comes from the word Kotleta which is Russian and means breaded meat products.

VEAL BRASCIOLI ALLA SICILIANA

My zia Pina's recipe, updated by Carmela

SERVES: 2

INGREDIENTS

> 3 x 200g veal schnitzels (without crumbs and tenderised, sliced into 4 or 5 small pieces)
> 2 cups bacon (diced)
> 150g butter (diced)
> 2 cups Mozzarella (diced)

COATING

> Breadcrumbs
> ½ cup parsley (chopped)
> Drizzle of virgin olive oil

PREPARATION TIME: about 20 minutes

COOKING TIME: about 15 minutes

EQUIPMENT YOU WILL NEED

Chopping board

Meat tenderiser

Oven tray

Chopping knife

2 Skewers

METHOD GRILL/BBQ

Place the veal onto a chopping board, then add about 6 pieces of diced bacon on top of each piece along with a tablespoon of Mozzarella and half a teaspoon of butter. Roll the veal and place onto a skewer. Continue to do this until you have at least 6 to 8 pieces of veal on each skewer. Roll the skewered veal in the breadcrumb mixture and either grill or barbeque them. Serve with a salad.

(After slicing your veal you can mix it with a little oil and salt and pepper to keep it nice and moist.)

TIP: With this meal you can replace the veal with chicken. However if you choose chicken, use cheddar cheese, as it gives the chicken a more intense flavour. You could also use beef, another versatile and tasty meat.

These are my favourite veal dishes (I used to cook them at my zia Pina's house (my mum's sister) in Milazzo, on her balcony using a fire grill). You can prepare them in advance and then freeze. When you have unexpected guests you can take them out of the freezer and really impress. They are a type of street food in Sicily. I have added more ingredients that have blended well with this recipe.

When you have unexpected guests you can take them out of the freezer and really impress.

Saltimbocca (also salinbocca), which in Italian means jumps in the mouth, is made up of veal lined or topped with prosciutto and sage or basil, and marinated in wine, oil or salt water depending on the region. Every region in Italy has their own way of preparing it dish according to their taste.

SALTIMBOCCA

Carmela's Cucina Povera recipe

SERVES: 2

INGREDIENTS

- 8 baby veal pieces
- 4 slices prosciutto
- Sage
- Flour for coating
- Olive oil
- Butter
- 3 tablespoons of Dry White Wine

PREPARATION TIME: about 15 minutes

COOKING TIME: about 10 minutes

EQUIPMENT YOU WILL NEED

Large frying pan

Medium chopping board

Medium chopping knife

METHOD STOVETOP

Place the veal onto a board and beat with a tenderiser. Put the fresh sage on the top of the veal. Next, cut the prosciutto in half, placing it on top of each piece of veal. Then coat the veal with flour and place onto a clean board. Add the olive oil and butter to a frying pan and allow to sizzle.

When the butter has evaporated, place the veal in the pan and cook on a medium heat. Add a little wine and turn the veal over. As veal is very tender, it doesn't take long to cook, only about 2 to 3 minutes each side. Make sure that there is plenty of juice in this dish – the veal has a tendency to soak it all up. To make it super moist, add a ladle of stock or water and it will make its own sauce nice and thick.

This dish is also occasionally topped with capers depending on the individual's taste. You can play around with it according to what you like. You can also add black mammoth olives and/or a little gravy. Oh, my! So much! I am getting excited!

STUFFED EGGPLANTS OR RED CAPSICUM

"Family like branches on a tree, we all grow in different directions, yet our roots remain as one."
Author unknown

To me eggplants and red peppers are the most essential fruit in my kitchen. They have depth and warmth, are versatile and you can do almost anything with them. They can be grown in your garden or you can buy them at your local market. They are seasonal fruit, but you can usually get them all year-round.

ESSENTIAL SECRET INGREDIENTS
Smell the fruit, cook with love and play Italian music.

MELANZANI RIPIENI (STUFFED EGGPLANTS)

My mother Sarina's recipe, updated by Carmela

SERVES: 3

INGREDIENTS

- 4 cups cooked Arborio rice
- 6 medium eggplants
- 1 carrot (grated)
- 1 red onion (grated)
- 1 garlic clove (crushed)
- ½ kg pork mince (coarse)
- 2 cups Mozzarella (diced)
- 2 handfuls Parmesan/Romano
- ½ cup parsley (diced)
- 2 litres cooked Napoli sauce (see page 127)
- 2 cans tomatoes (diced)
- Handful of basil leaves
- Olive oil
- Salt/pepper to taste

PREPARATION TIME: about 30 minutes

COOKING TIME: about 2 hours

Preheat a 200°C oven for 20 minutes

EQUIPMENT YOU WILL NEED

Oven tray - Chopping board - Chopping knife

Paring knife - Spoon - Mixing bowl

METHOD BENCHTOP/OVEN

Cut the tops off the eggplants and use a spoon to remove the meat. And discard. Place the tops to one side so you can use them like a hat to help hold the filling in with toothpicks.

Place the cooked rice, pork, tomatoes, Mozzarella, Parmesan, parsley, basil leaves, garlic, onion and carrots into a mixing bowl and mix with your hands. Add some oil and season to taste. Next, place the filling into the eggplants, adding the tops using toothpicks on either side to help secure the filling.

Then, place onto a baking tray, top them with Napoli sauce and place into the preheated oven. Cook for about one and a half hours at 180°C. Keep an eye on the Mozzarella as it could burn. If preferred you can substitute red capsicums for the eggplants.

TIP: You can prepare the eggplants and red capsicums in a number of different ways. You can cut both the eggplants and rec capsicums in half, scoop out the meat/seeds, then add the filling and place onto a baking tray with greaseproof paper. You can finish them with grated Mozzarella cheese and Parmesan on top, place in the oven and allow to cook for about 1½ hours. Make sure that the oven is only at 180°C, as the Mozzarella cheese could burn.

PART FOUR

TRAILBLAZING:

CELEBRATING THE NEW GENERATION

"Do not go where the path may lead, go instead where there is no path and leave a trail."

.... Ralph Waldo Emerson.

MAKING MY OWN TRAIL

Trail means path, road, route, mark, track and way

Over the course of my life, I have blazed my own trail. Today, my children are blazing their own trails and so are my grandchildren. I believe it's important that elements of my Sicilian and Australian culture are interwoven into the fabric of my family and their families.

Leaving my own cultural footprint

I realised how important leaving cultural footprints was to me when my mother passed away. At that time I asked myself what I wanted to leave behind for the next few generations. What I really want to leave behind for my children and grandchildren is love, family, strength, determination, gratitude and my own principles (see page 207). I want them to be able to face their own journey and know that those before them also faced many other obstacles - that through my obstacles, I did not give up, I continued and persevered.

I want my children to have time to grow and evolve and take time to find their own roots and become strong and confident.

I have learnt to take the best from my culture and to discard what doesn't work for me and recognise that all cultures have good and bad elements.

There is a saying: "A leader is one who goes the way, shows the way and knows the way".

Facing my own demons

I and many women from my generation with my cultural background have faced drug problems, addictions, death, separation and many other personal trials. These are problems that have passed on through to the next generation.

I needed to find the courage within me to give my family the important human quality of strength to pass on to the next generation. I did not have those tools when I was growing up. It took time and many life lessons to find them. Like an explorer along the way, seek and you shall find.

Digging deep to find the strength to carry on

Sometimes I had to dig so deep that I thought I would die. And die I did! I died and restored myself to a new being, a brand new person. Throughout this evolutionary process, I had to face all of my demons that I had created from earlier in my life. I found that by changing my perception of the world I was able to change my reality.

By facing my demons, changing my perception and sharing what I learned from other women of my culture, I discovered that they too had very similar experiences growing up in Australia.

Coming to terms with personal rebellion and pushing my parents' boundaries

I was a very rebellious teenager. My parents didn't have the tools to deal with my behaviour. They did not have the tools to manage my generation. I rebelled through most of my teens and did the exact opposite to what I was supposed to do.

In telling you this, there was a deep down sense of me wanting them to acknowledge who I was and to allow me the freedom to become the person I was born to be.

They were afraid. Fear drove them. All they knew was how to work and give us a roof over our head and give us a clear path to education.

I deeply loved my parents and I would never change them for the world. I told them that every day, because they were my teachers and I was their pupil. I learnt the lessons the hard way and in doing that I am grateful every day, because, they are embedded into my being. They taught me to be the person I am today.

My parents brought their old ways to this country. As the saying goes, you cannot put old wine into new wine skins. It's impossible and it will destroy the wine. If you aren't given a manual and you don't know how to operate the machinery, you just go by what you think and you can really harm yourself. You can slice a limb or a hand. If you have been educated and taught how to operate the machinery, you will learn to master it and become a professional.

REVISITING THE THREE BIGGEST CHALLENGES I FACED AND THE MISTAKES THAT STEMMED FROM THEM

Through my own extensive research and personal experience, I identified that the generation of women that I come from faced many different problems with their children: drug problems, alcohol addictions and death. Their experiences have put a dent in the next generation.

I believe a dent in the earth needs to be fixed. Otherwise, it will hurt the entire earth.

Through communication and my solid principles, I have found that slowly I have planted seeds of hope and found a light through the darkness.

Without communication and changing old mindsets, it would continue to grow into an uncontrollable force throughout future generations. Without trying to find a solution to the problem, either I am part of the solution or I become part of the problem - to me there is no in between.

So how do I fix this, when I am just one person?

I decided to do it by starting with myself. And in doing that, I have seen a trail come through – glimpses of hope, love, change, the shifting of the generation of acceptance.

There have been many questions that have gone through my mind and several decades of asking 'why'?

The journeys of my children and cultural mindsets

Observing my own children and the issues that several of them had with drugs and alcohol, I asked myself what could I have done to prevent the problems that they faced. I asked myself how I could extend my hand to help them cross their own frontiers – and to face their own demons.

They are questions that I cannot give you full answers for today because each one of us is an individual and we each make our own choices in life. That is our journey.

In making my own life choices, I could choose the right path or I could choose to remain ignorant. Through baby steps and with an interest in being a better person, I have gained the courage to be as flexible as I can - to change like bamboo, stretching and weathering the storms and sometimes blizzards and hurricanes in my life.

There is an old saying, "give a person a fish and you feed them for a day; teach them how to fish you feed them for life". Another is, "change one child and you change the entire village".

I have decided through my learning that changing is like the weather. We have to accept it (accetare), otherwise if we whinge and complain, the day has been wasted. If we accept that it is raining, then we take a raincoat and go out anyway. If it's sunny we need sunglasses and hats otherwise the sun will burn us.

Confronting my inner darkness

Throughout my life, darkness has kept me captive. I have had my own battle with depression. I could not see that my own children were facing their own struggles. By eventually awakening my inner courage, I finally stepped out of my comfort zone, one day at a time. It changed the direction in which I was travelling.

When I realised where I was at, I recognised that I could not change the way things were, but I could change my attitude to what was going on around me. In doing that, I built a life of happiness and gratitude. Baby steps again maybe, but choosing every day to be a better person – some days are better than others.

Recognising that happiness is a journey

I realise that happiness is not a destination. I fall down, but I pick myself up. It is no longer impossible. The bad days are simply speed bumps. Thinking this way gives me the strength to persevere and to put into action what
I know now.

I recognised that I needed professional help. I recognised that I was not an expert in what was happening to me. I reached a precipice in my life and it was a case of change or die.

Fixing me

My mum and dad were passing away and I finally came to a realisation that I needed to fix me and find help.

The exact minute and time I remember because it was an event that changed the whole entire course of my life. When I decided that I needed help, I found a professional, who knew how to help me and get me out of the mindset that I was in.

It has taken a few years and I still go to see him for a tune-up, as I am a human being who is always evolving and needing guidance during my journey. I learnt that if I want to be in this world, I have to start living in it, not just existing on autopilot.

Having a marathon runner mindset

I think of life as though I am a marathon runner. A marathon runner doesn't just decide to start running. They undertake and build-up an exercise regime. They have a daily routine of checking their health, their diet, their mindset and continuously practising and finding what works for his or her body.

I put this into practice in my daily life and it is a daily choice of knowing what does or doesn't work for me. The choice is mine. There is a saying in Italian, that goes, "Chi va piano va Lontano" which means he who goes slowly goes a long way.

Thinking of my life as a masterpiece

My life is like a masterpiece in the making and I choose if I want it to be distorted or a magnificent piece in the making.

If I want it to be a masterpiece then I will leave a priceless trail for the generations to come. If I want it to look like a distorted piece then that is what I leave behind. The earth is my school ground and it is where I learn my lessons to become whoever and whatever I choose. Regardless of my circumstances I have to choose to get up and do my best, regardless of what comes my way and slowly, over time, my life will transform itself and the perfect masterpiece will take shape.

Today I am creating a masterpiece so that the generations to come can see the trail of my life, which embodies a love of my culture, a love of who I am, a love of life and the best of me.

I've seen people rise from tragedies and become mentors and people who had nothing become an inspiration to others. I want to be that inspiration. To blaze a trail.

LOOKING AFTER MY HEALTH

ESSENTIAL SECRET INGREDIENTS

A willing heart to look after yourself

A positive attitude

Smile when you exercise

Listen to your favourite music

> "Every journey begins with a single step."
> *Maya Angelou*

I exercise regularly and eat healthily. In doing that, I strive to have a healthy mind and soul, which is important. With a balance of these attributes, I think better, feel better and act better every day.

Eight tips for healthy eating carmela's cucina way:

1. I base my meals on starchy foods.

I pick foods like bread, potatoes, pasta, rice and noodles. Choose whole grains, potatoes and sweet potatoes with the skin on where possible, as they contain more fibre, vitamins and minerals. Starchy foods contain fewer than half the calories of fats per gram.

2. I eat plenty of fruit and vegetables.

I always choose seasonal produce and a wide variety of fruit and vegetables as they contain many different combinations of vitamins and minerals. Fresh fruit is the best. Buy what's in season. Add grated vegetables, like carrots and zucchini, and celery to your pasta sauces or lots of vegetables to homemade tomato sauce.

3. **I eat more fish and aim for at least two portions per week.**

I use one of those oily fish, such as salmon, fresh tuna, sardines, mackerel or trout. Note that one portion of fish is approximately 140g cooked. Oily fish are an excellence source of vitamin D which is important for bone health. You can choose from fresh, smoked or canned but remember smoked fish and often canned fish, contains salt. Where possible, I check the labels and choose those with lower salt content.

4. **I cut down on saturated fats and sugar.**

Although I need some fat in my diet (to provide the essential fatty acids and aid the absorption of the fat soluble vitamins A, D, E and K), too much fat may lead to weight gain. Fat provides nine calories per gram, more than double that from carbohydrates and protein. I replace saturated fats from butter, lard, pastries, cream, pies and cheese (which can increase my blood cholesterol levels) with unsaturated fats found in vegetable oil, nuts, seeds, oily fish and avocadoes.

5. **I eat less salt.**

High salt intake is associated with an increased risk of developing high blood pressure that puts me at a greater risk of developing heart disease. As I age, I tend to put more weight on and going through menopause I need to exercise more, as my body becomes sluggish.

6. **My goal every day is to be active and maintain a healthy weight.**

I need to walk or exercise at least five to six times a week. Walking is an ideal form of exercise as it does not place much strain on my body and I can walk fast, sprint, jog, or run some of the way.

Walking is a non-negotiable activity of mine. I make it a point to get up early and try to go to bed early, as my health is so important. I walk four kilometres a day. It helps me to think more clearly and gives me more energy.

I was not always this healthy, but I made it my goal to get to this point. I took baby steps. Every day I went a little further and I have tried to jog, but have not made it to running. I love to see women running. They look so happy and healthy. I am spoilt living on the Mornington Peninsula, as I get to see the beach every day and it makes me feel at one with the universe – looking at the scenery is truly a blessing.

7. **I try to drink plenty of water.**

My goal is to drink at least eight to ten glasses per day. Water hydrates me without adding calories. Coconut water is another liquid that I add to my drinking. Cooking in the kitchen dehydrates me, so I like to have a change and drink coconut water. I add it to my diet as it provides calcium, magnesium, phosphorous, sodium and potassium in their natural form and a little carbohydrate. The fresher the better.

8. **I never, ever skip breakfast!**

Breakfast gives me the kick-start to thinking healthily and being healthy. A healthy breakfast is the fuel for my day. I choose gluten-free cereals, porridge or grain toast. I make lots of smoothies with seasonal fruit, goji berries, honey and almond milk.

I have invested in a Nutriblast. I add protein to my smoothies with flaxseed oil or almonds. I also add hazelnuts and buy protein powder at my local supermarket or my health food store.

SELF-HEALING THROUGH THE ART OF COOKING

> "Let food be thy medicine and medicine be thy food."
> *Hippocrates*

ESSENTIAL SECRET INGREDIENTS

A willingness to change

An open heart

Embracing life and loving

I have found that doing what you love to do is the best thing in life that there is. What the secret recipe is to discovering it is a mystery, but I am a willing pupil.

For me, cooking is both creative and healing. Cooking allows me—and you—to create and at the same time, think unconsciously about what is going on inside.

Cooking is a great de-stresser because it activates my senses through aroma, taste, touch and visual delight – and it gives me a creative outlet. With every dish I get to begin again. Every dish I create is like a new birth. Stress, on the other hand, numbs your senses.

When I'm cooking for people I care about, I am gratified by their appreciation. Cooking for people I love is one of the most soothing experiences I know. Just seeing their faces is so rewarding.

Cooking also helps me to feel better about life, because it offers me immediate gratification, keeping me in the moment and shifting my attention from worry to a delicious recipe for a happy meal.

Cooking is the fastest way to mend a broken heart. It heals and soothes the nerves and cures boredom, insomnia and anxiety.

Research suggests that certain fragrances soothe and relieve stress. Among them are lemon, mango and lavender. Simply cut open a lemon and take a big whiff while you are cooking and it opens your senses, Peppermint also perks you up.

It contains something that gives you energy and helps to soothe an upset stomach as well.

Discovering the art of cooking I have been able to heal myself. I have consoled myself through my own cultural journey – discovering my foundations. Embracing my love of Cucina Povera.

I'm teaching my children and the people around me to find the good in their culture and to embrace the changes that future generations bring, even if those changes may appear strange and unfamiliar.

FOOD INTOLERANCES

My own experiences with food Intolerances

I'll start by stating that a food allergy is completely different from food intolerance.

A food allergy involves an immune system response, while food intolerance does not.

I have been diagnosed with some food intolerances during the last decades that have stopped me from being able to digest certain foods.

If you have food intolerances you cannot properly digest a substance in certain foods, often because you have an enzyme deficiency. That is what I have been told by professionals.

Food allergies however have nothing to do with enzyme deficiencies. The symptoms associated with food allergies appear soon after eating particular foods. A person with a food allergy cannot tolerate even small amounts of that food, as is the case with peanuts. A protein causes an allergic reaction, an immune response. An allergen is a protein that causes a food allergy.

Food intolerance symptoms, on the other hand, appear later. Generally a very small amount of the food can be consumed with no adverse reaction.

> "Happiness is a good bank account, a good cook, and a good digestion."
> *John Jacques Rousseau*

Food allergies and food intolerance: the symptoms

The symptoms of allergic reactions to foods are generally seen on the skin (hives, itchiness, swelling of the skin). Gastrointestinal symptoms may include vomiting and diarrhoea. Respiratory symptoms may accompany skin and gastrointestinal symptoms, but don't usually occur alone.

The main symptoms associated with food intolerance are intestinal gas, abdominal pain or diarrhoea. Other symptoms are also possible, but the ones related to problems with the gut are the core symptoms.

Allergies and intolerances: the everyday foods that cause them

Common foods that cause allergic reactions: Eggs, fish, groundnuts, peanuts, milk, tree nuts Brazil nuts, walnuts, almonds and hazelnuts, shellfish and wheat.

Common foods that cause intolerance: Beans, cabbage, citrus fruit, grains containing gluten, milk (lactose) and processed meats.

What is lactose intolerance?

People with lactose intolerance cannot metabolise lactose properly. They lack lactase and the enzyme required in the digestive system to break down lactose. Typical symptoms include bloating, flatulence, abdominal cramps and diarrhoea after consuming food that contain lactose (such as milk or ice cream). Lactose is a sugar that is found in the milk of mammals. It makes up about two to eight per cent of milk. The human body uses the enzyme lactase to break down lactose into glucose, which is then absorbed into the bloodstream.

I recommend Zymil milk, from Pauls.

If you think you may be lactose intolerant, get tested by a professional. You usually receive a hydrogen breath test and a lactose tolerance test. You will know straight away.

Understanding gluten intolerance

A gluten-free diet requires the removal of numerous food sources. There is more to it than removing wheat from your diet.

People diagnosed with coeliac disease have an intolerance to dietary gluten. Gluten is the protein component of wheat, rye, barley and oats and is present in many foods made from these.

When people with coeliac disease eat foods containing gluten, their immune system responds by damaging the villi in the small intestine. This causes inflammation and flattening of the villi, which can seriously deplete the surface area of the small intestine and therefore reduce the absorption of nutrients.

Symptoms of coeliac disease can include diarrhoea or constipation or a combination of both, flatulence, bloating, abdominal pain and fatigue. It can also cause other conditions such as nausea, nutritional deficiencies, including folate deficiencies, osteoporosis, bowel cancer and infertility.

What to avoid on a gluten-free diet

You will need to avoid wheat (all varieties including spelt, durum, kumat and dinkel), barley, oats, triticale and derivatives of these products such as malt, biscuits, cakes and pastry products.

Gluten may also be present in other foods such as confectionery, smallgoods, sauces, dressings and other condiments. Malted and cereal drinks, yeast extract spreads and many others may also contain gluten.

Gluten-free grains and starches include corn (maize), rice, soy, polenta, potato, tapioca, buckwheat, psyllium, sago, millet, amaranth, seeds, lentil, lupin and quinoa. I am just touching on this subject. It is so big that I could write another book about it.

NOTE: Always seek professional help if you are suffering from any condition that could affect your health. Once I sought professional help and found out what I could and couldn't eat, I had guidelines that allowed me to have control over my health.

Essential secret ingredients
Family, heritage and love.

SWEETS

Il Dolce far niente: the sweetness of doing nothing

Sicilians love sweets. It's just a part of our culture. We even have sweets for breakfast! We have a cup of espresso and a sweet biscuit to start our day. I know it's not very nutritious, but it's just part of the European diet.

We have brioche with granita (made up from fresh lemons, sugar and water and you can even add liqueurs) for breakfast in the summer. We have panettone for Easter and Christmas with our breakfast and for winter we have a cornetto (Italian croissant) or a sfogliatella (sweet ricotta filled pastry) with an espresso. This is one that I have had to keep for special occasions only, as my health is important. I enjoy eating what I was brought up with. Because of my culture and the way we eat, I like to give myself a treat, so I do this only at Easter and Christmas time, as it is important for me to continue eating healthily.

I had to include the recipe below because it is a timeless. There are Arabian influences in the flavours of this cake. This famous sponge cake is filled with ricotta and decorated with green pistachio nuts and almond paste. Sometimes it's glazed with a thin layer of icing so that the green colour shines through and it's topped with candied fruits.
(Refer to Cassata Recipe page 198)

Tiramisu means 'pull me up'. Its inventor was the confectioner Roberto Linguanotto. He owned a restaurant called Le Beccherie in Treviso, Italy, where his god-daughter Francesca Valori worked as an apprentice. In honour of her culinary skills he wanted to make a dessert for her and so he made the world famous dessert and named it after her maiden name Francesca Valori-Tiramisu.

In traditional pastry, tiramisu has similarities with cakes like Zuppa Inglese which is an Italian custard-based trifle made with ladyfinger biscuits. I also like to add canned peaches. And you can dunk the ladyfinger biscuits in liqueur.

The word zuppa in Italian cuisine refers to both sweet and savoury dishes. It comes from the verb inzuppare, which means to dunk. As the sponge cake or ladyfingers are dipped in liqueur, the dish is called zuppa.

This is another example of how creative we can be and make do with what we have, through another Cucina Povera recipe.

One of the best things about tiramisu is its versatility. Though the conventional version calls for espresso soaked Savoiardi (ladyfinger biscuits), I have found that you can blend other flavours into this magnificent dessert.

It's great for big family gatherings: I can make it for 2 or 20 and it can be stretched and adapted to how far I want it to go!

TIRAMISU AL LIMONCELLO

Carmela's Cucina Povera recipe

INGREDIENTS

- 5 or 6 lemons
- 5 large eggs
- 1 cup sugar
- 1½ cups Limoncello liqueur
- 1 cup water
- 2 cups mascarpone (room temperature)
- 40 Savoiardi biscotti

PREPARATION TIME: about 30 minutes

REFRIGERATION TIME: about 6 hours-2 days

EQUIPMENT YOU WILL NEED

Grater - Double boiler pan - 2 large stainless steel bowls

2 ceramic bowls - Medium saucepan - Pyrex dish

Egg whisk - Wooden spoon - Rubber spatula

METHOD STOVETOP

Use a grater to remove the zest from two or more lemons, so that you have 2 tablespoons of zest. Squeeze all the lemons and strain the juice to get three-quarters of a cup of fresh lemon juice and set aside. >>>>

Meanwhile, pour water into a double boiler pan so that the water level sits just below the bottom of the mixing bowl when it is on top of the pan. Bring to the boil and allow to simmer, then set aside.

Separate the eggs, placing the yolks into the large bowl of the double boiler and the whites into a separate stainless steel bowl.

Beat the egg yolks with a quarter of a cup of sugar and half a cup of Limoncello until it's well blended. Place the bowl over the simmering water and whisk constantly, frequently scraping the whisk around the sides and bottom of the bowl, as the egg mixture expands and heats into a frothy sponge. This should take about 5 minutes or so.

When the base of the sponge has thickened enough to form a ribbon when it drops onto the surface, take the bowl off the double boiler pan and allow to cool.

Meanwhile, pour into a saucepan the remaining cup of Limoncello, all the lemon juice, one cup of water and half a cup of the sugar and bring to the boil, stirring to dissolve the sugar. Cook for 5 minutes, evaporating the alcohol, then let the syrup cool completely. This is called Limoncello zabaglione.

In a ceramic bowl, stir the mascarpone with a wooden spoon to soften it, then add the lemon zest and beat with a whisk until it becomes light and creamy.

When the Limoncello zabaglione is cooked, scrape about a third of it over the mascarpone and fold it in with a large rubber spatula. Fold in the rest of the zabaglione in two or three stages.

Whip the egg whites with the remaining quarter of a cup of sugar until it holds moderately firm peaks. Then, in several stages fold them into the Limoncello mascarpone cream until it is light and evenly blended.

Pour some of the cooled syrup into a pan, no deeper than a quarter of an inch, to moisten the ladyfingers, one at a time. Quickly roll a ladyfinger in the syrup. Repeat this step with each biscotto, making sure you keep it quick. If it soaks too much syrup, it will fall apart.

Quickly arrange some the moistened biscotti in neat tight rows on the bottom of the pyrex dish, until the it is completely covered. Scoop half of the Limoncello mascarpone cream onto the biscotti and smooth to cover them. Dip and arrange a second layer of the biscotti in the dish and cover completely with the remainder of the cream. Smooth the cream with the spatula and seal the tiramisu airtight in cling wrap.

Refrigerate the dish for 6 hours or up to 2 days. Or if you're in a hurry, freeze it for 2 hours.

Scoop out portions of the tiramisu onto dessert plates and serve them with cold espresso coffee. Delicious on a hot day!

CASSATA SICILIANA

Carmela's Cucina Povera recipe

There are so many types of cassata; it also refers to the ice cream that is made from candied sweet fruits. Another classic is the cannoli with ricotta.

INGREDIENTS

- 900g good quality fresh ricotta
- 400g caster sugar
- 100ml cherry liqueur
- 150g candied fruit (chopped)
- 150g chocolate chips (chopped)
- 24cm round plain sponge cake
- 2 tablespoons apricot jam, heated until melted

TO DECORATE

- 100g pistachios
- 300g golden marzipan
- 300g icing sugar, plus extra for dusting
- Whole candied fruit

PREPARATION TIME: about 40-50 minutes

Preheat a 180°C oven for 20 minutes

COOKING TIME: about 5 minutes

REFRIGERATION TIME: about 1 to 2 hours before serving

EQUIPMENT YOU WILL NEED

Baking tray

Blender or food processor

Ceramic mixing bowl

Bowl – around 5cm deep with sloping sides

Cake serving plate

Wooden spoon

Cling wrap

METHOD OVEN

Preheat the oven to 180°C. Lay the pistachios in a single layer on a baking tray and bake in the oven for about 8 minutes. As long as they are in a single layer you don't need to turn them. Keep a close eye on them as they can burn. Next, place them into a blender and blitz until the nuts release their oil. You will now have a paste similar in density to melted chocolate.

Place the marzipan into another bowl and with your hands work in the pistachio paste until the paste is bright green. Dust your work surface with icing sugar and roll out the paste into a strip that is as deep as the sides of the bowl you are going to make the cassata in. Put the strip of paste to one side.

Find a bowl that is about 5cm deep, preferably with sloping sides and line it with cling wrap. You will need this when you're making the cassata.

In another bowl, add the ricotta, sugar, liqueur, candied fruit and chocolate chips and mix together.

Meanwhile, heat the apricot jam in a small saucepan over a low heat until it melts.

PREPARING THE SPONGE CAKE

Cut the sponge cake to form two discs, each about 1cm thick. Place one of the cake discs in the bottom of a bowl lined with cling wrap and brush lightly with some of the melted jam.

Line the sides of the bowl with strips of green marzipan. Spoon in the ricotta mixture and smooth the top to make it level and cover it with the remaining sponge cake disc. Refrigerate for at least 4 hours.

Next, place a plate on top of the bowl. Turn the plate and bowl over together, turning the cake out onto the plate. Remove the cling wrap.

MAKING THE GLAZE

Make the glaze by mixing the icing sugar with enough water to make it spreadable. Cover the top and sides with the sugar glaze – very thinly, so that you can see the green paste through it.

Decorate with candied fruit and return to the fridge for at least another hour before serving. This cake is a traditional Sicilian cake, it is timeless and the influence of Sicily comes out in the flavours.

SPINCHI - SFINGI (SICILIAN DONUTS)

My mother Sarina's recipe, updated by Carmela

This recipe is my mothers recipe that I updated and developed it from years of making these Sicilian donuts. My mum used to make a filling with ricotta as well but there are many ways of making them.

This is another recipe from Cucina Povera. You made do with what ingredients you had and made very flavoursome meals and desserts.

INGREDIENTS

- 1kg plain flour
- 1 cup sultanas
- 200g fresh yeast
- 2 cups caster sugar
- 1 cup cinnamon
- Teaspoon of salt
- 2 litres warm water
- Canola oil for frying

PREPARATION TIME: about 20 minutes

STANDING TIME FOR DOUGH TO RISE: about 3-4 hours

COOKING TIME: about 15 minutes

EQUIPMENT YOU WILL NEED

Mixing bowl - Ceramic mixing bowl - Measuring cup

Wooden spoon - Deep frying pan

METHOD STOVETOP

Place the flour, a 1 teaspoon of salt and 2 tablespoons of sugar with the sultanas into a mixing bowl.

In a separate bowl, add warm water to the yeast and mix with a wooden spoon. Next, add the flour mixture to the bowl containing the yeast and keep mixing with a wooden spoon, until the texture becomes really loose and easy to manage taking care not to use all of the water, it is only a guideline. If you need to, add more water. Allow it to sit for at least three to four hours in a warm place. This gives the dough time to rest and rise. Remember dough needs its own time to do its thing.

When the dough has risen, using your hands make balls with the dough mixture (about the size of a golf ball). The mixture is easier to work with if you wet your hands with water.

Heat the oil in a deep frying pan and add the dough balls, until they turn golden brown. Remove from the oil and roll them in a mixture of caster sugar and cinnamon. Serve with fresh cream and strawberries.

TIP: Dough is always at its best when it has had time to sit. You can make this mixture and put it in the fridge overnight. Use the next day and it will have a crunchier texture when you cook it.

FIG, RICOTTA AND HONEY PIZZA DESSERT

Carmela's Cucina Povera recipe

Do you have homemade pizza bases in the freezer already? You can use them with this recipe. If you need to make some fresh pizza bases, see the recipe on page 99.

INGREDIENTS

- 115g fresh ricotta
- 30ml icing sugar
- 6 ripe figs, sliced lengthwise
- 3 tablespoons honey
- Pre-made pizza base
- Ice cream

PREPARATION TIME: about 15 minutes

COOKING TIME: about 20 minutes

Preheat a 230°C oven for 20 minutes

EQUIPMENT YOU WILL NEED

Pizza stone

Food processor or stick mixer

Wire rack

Chopping knife

METHOD BENCHTOP/OVEN

Place a pizza stone on the middle rack of your oven, preheated to 230°C.

In a food processor, mix the ricotta and sugar until it becomes smooth. Spread the ricotta mixture over the pre-made pizza base, arrange the figs and drizzle with honey. Place in the oven and bake for about 12 to 15 minutes, until the base is slightly puffy and golden brown.

Remove the pizza from the oven and transfer to the wire rack to cool. Serve with ice cream.

ESPRESSO COFFEE

Any Sicilian/Italian will always have a coffee, we do not have to have an excuse to have one. It is just the way we have been brought up. A coffee complements a meal. It invites a friend to share a conversation with you and while you are having a coffee, you can relax. It's a way of telling you to stop for a while and just sit, with yourself, a friend, or a loved one. Today we are becoming more social and enjoying meeting friends or family at our local café and sitting outside being very European.

My experience is that the best coffee beans are usually made up of 70 per cent Arabica and 30 per cent Robusta. In Sicily the average blend is 49 per cent Arabica and 51 per cent Robusta. In Sicily the cappuccino and latte are not served with boiling milk, but is served warm for you to savour and enjoy.

Essential secret ingredients
Good conversation
Being social
Being with a great friend
Having time out

Coffee is the crowning glory of a Sicilian meal and the aroma of the espresso is savoured throughout the evening and just lingers on your palate.

A brief history of coffee

The Arabs introduced coffee to Italy in the 17th century. They had discovered that their goats got a lot of energy from eating the berries and leaves of the coffee plant. This formed the basis for the practice of making coffee that was established by the Arabs.

When the first café opened on the Piazza San Marco in Venice in 1675, the oriental drink caught on immediately. However, it was considered an unchristian drink. There were even calls to ban it! Nevertheless when Pope Clement VII tried the drink for himself, he gave his permission as he did not want to deny the Catholics coffee, so he said, "we will conquer the devil by baptising the drink and turning it into a Christian product."

It wasn't long before there was a coffee house on almost every street.

Today, there are more than 200,000 coffee bars all around Italy and the number continues to grow. Nowadays, there are still more cafés in Sicily/Italy than in the whole of Europe. Even in the smallest villages you will find an espresso machine switched on. Sicilians/Italians love to go out for a cup of coffee. It's a way of life. You will find Sicilian/Italians standing up in the bar talking and having their coffee. They will savour it and enjoy the company of their friends. My husband Marco has about 15 coffees a day. If I take the coffee from him he will die! He loves coffee and enjoys every cup.

Other ways to enjoy a coffee

There is more than one way to have a cup of coffee. You can add grappa to it or you can have an affogato, which is an espresso coffee with liqueur and vanilla ice cream.

> "The best thing about me waking up, is knowing that an espresso awaits me. It gives me great joy to start my day."
>
> — Carmela

My mother's story

My mother used to tell me that when people would visit our family home, she would bring out the sweets and the liqueurs and people would sit and chat for hours.

Hours later you would be able to smell the aroma of the coffee percolator. Coffee was the last thing given to visitors. It was used as a sign that it was time to go. You never made coffee first. It was taboo. If you did, your guests thought that you did not want their visit and they would leave earlier.

Suggestions for coffee machines or percolators

For a stovetop coffee percolator I use a the Bialetti two-cup machine. It is usually around $30. This make has been around for as long as I can remember and is a really good brand. There are so many that you can choose from, if you want to look at other brands. You can buy them at your local hospitality or homewares store, or at your local Italian supermarket.

We make so many coffees in my home, that my husband Marco bought a Saeco machine about 15 years ago and every five years, he buys a new one. They start at around $1,000 but they are a good investment for coffee lovers. We make latte cappuccinos and espresso – this is a daily routine in our household.

I cannot tell you how many coffees are made in my home.

CELEBRATING THE NEXT GENERATION

"Winners are the people who, when the odds are stacked against them, and those around them have fallen, will have the courage to look within themselves and make the unbelievable believable, and the impossible possible." - C. Phillips

ESSENTIAL SECRET INGREDIENTS

Making time for a loved one, enjoying time with them, laughter and family.

....

THE NEXT GENERATION

Looking into the eyes of the next generation, I see a future packed with hope and prosperity in a land overflowing with new possibilities. I know for certain that this life and the lives of my grandchildren will be full of challenges and curve balls, much like the roads travelled before them.

My grandchildren already associate me with cooking and gardening. They say, "Nonna, what are you cooking?" They love the garden, just like me. They like to plant and see seeds grow, like my parents and grandparents did.

It's amazing how you see glimpses of everyone that you have loved and remembered, in the future generation. Like every grandparent, I want to make sure that the lives of my grandchildren are going to be okay. You also know that they will make their own way and find their own path and you hope that during their journey they want to lean on you for help and guidance.

You may predict their future and the journey that's ahead of them and hope that they draw strength from what you have taught them about having hope, courage and strength.

Their future is full of whatever they choose to make of it. Likewise, like the future generations we mustn't lose sight of the fact that even though we're older, we too can choose how we want to live, where we want to live and who we want to live it with as well as the kind of friends we want.

Every new generation that emerges has a chance to make the world a better place, by embracing what works well and discarding what doesn't. The universe we live in regenerates every day and every day each and every person has a chance to do it right.

PRINCIPLES

"Optimism is essential to achievement and it is also the foundation of courage and true progress." - Nicholas Murray Butler

ESSENTIAL SECRET INGREDIENTS

Courage, love, and laughter.

....

I have principles that I live by, each and every day on this earth.
I have created an acronym from words that represent the principles that I live by.

The acronym that I have created, and want to leave with you, is **C.O.U.R.A.G.E.**

These letters represent the traits of human kindness. They are essential life ingredients for me.

COMMUNICATION, OPTIMISM, UNDERSTANDING, RELATIONSHIPS, ACCEPTANCE, GENTLENESS AND EMPATHY

Without **COMMUNICATION,** I cannot tell you what I want or let you know what is going on with me.

Without having **OPTIMISM** I cannot look upon my life or the future. I need to be positive and share that energy with family and strangers. Life is what I make of it and how I see it.

UNDERSTANDING is a word that can change my life. If I choose to understand myself and others, we have met half way and can see each other's viewpoint.

When it comes to **RELATIONSHIPS,** I am not an island. I need friends, family, my children and strangers. We are all connected in this world. We all live in it and are part of it. To reach out to others and make a relationship with the people around me is a gift from me to them.

ACCEPTANCE. To accept; to accetare, gives me more freedom in this world than any word I know. With acceptance comes the freedom to be more of myself and accept more of others.

GENTLENESS is a word that I have needed most of my life. I have been hard on myself and hard on others. It has been a journey to get to gentleness. I am now gentle with friends, family, strangers and the universe, but mostly with myself.

EMPATHY refers to the capacity for participating in feeling what others feel. It's about putting myself in another person's shoes and understanding why they do what they do and understanding them.

AUSTRALIA

"Because the time has come, well and truly come, for all peoples of our great country, for all citizens of our great commonwealth, for all Australians - those who are indigenous and those who are not - to come together to reconcile and together build a new future for our nation." - Kevin Rudd

ESSENTIAL SECRET INGREDIENTS

Loving your home. Love your country. Loving your family. Loving friends. Loving yourself

Australia is one of the wealthiest countries in the world and home to the world's twelfth largest economy.

The name Australia is derived from the Latin Australis, meaning southern, however the country has been referred to colloquially as 'Oz' since the early 20th century.

The name Australia was popularised by the explorer Matthew Flinders, who pushed for the name to be formally adopted as early as 1804. When preparing his manuscript and charts for his 1814 `(a) voyage to Terra Australis' he was persuaded by his patron Sir Joseph Banks to use the term Terra Australis, as this was the name most familiar to the public. Flinders did so and published the following rationale:

"This is no probability, that any other detached body of land, of nearly equal extent, will ever be found in a more southern latitude. The name Terra Australis will, therefore, remain descriptive of the geographical importance of this country, and of its situation on the globe: it has antiquity to recommend it; and, having no reference to either of the two claiming nations, appears to be less objectionable than any other which could have been selected. Had I permitted myself any innovation on the original term, it would have been to convert it to Australia; as being more agreeable to the ear and assimilation to the names of the other great portions of the earth."

MY FAVOURITE POEM ABOUT AUSTRALIA

My Country by Dorothea Mackellar, takes me back to my school days. I remember reciting it and falling in love with the words. Dorothea's poem has power in every word, to show me about the big wide country and the beauty in what she (Australia) holds. I see what she means, about how beautiful Australia is.

I recited it at primary school and have never forgotten it. I remember placing my hand on my heart and as a young child, I knew my own foundations were here in Australia. Being born here made me proud, as I was given an opportunity for a future.

A future to make a life for my family and not have to face what my own parents and grandparents faced leaving their own country to set sail for another world and make a new life not knowing what was before them. I feel blessed to be called Australian. Here in Australia, I have been given the opportunity to learn, to be educated, to find choices. I found freedom, I created my own trail. The wealth of my country gave me freedom to be an authentic human being and the freedom to share my heritage with others and find healing through the art of cooking.

I am proud to call Australia my home. I love Australia and the only way I can tell you how much I love it, is by sharing this poem, leaving you with the most beautiful words that describe my country.

I have a deep love for Australia. It gave my parents, me and the next generations a home. She embraced us with unconditional love. She adopted us like a mother. She made room for us and for many more. I can go anywhere in the world, but Australia is my home – and it will always call me back, like this poem.

> The love of field and coppice,
> Of green and shaded lanes
> Of ordered woods and gardens,
> Is running in your veins
> Strong love of grey-blue distance,
> Brown streams and soft dim skies
> I know, but cannot share it,
> My love is otherwise,
> I love a sunburnt country,
> A land of sweeping plains,
> Of ragged mountain rangers
> Of droughts and flooding rains,
> I love her far horizons,
> I love her jewel sea,
> Her beauty and her terror
> The wide brown land for me!
> The stark white ring-barked forest,
> All tragic to the moon,
> The sapphire-misted mountains,
> The hot gold hush of noon
> Green tangle of the brushes,
> Where lithe lianas coil,
> And orchids deck the treetops,
> And ferns the warm dark soil
>
> Core of my heart, my country!
> Her pitiless blue sky,
> When sick at heart around us
> We see the cattle die
> But then the grey clouds gather,
> And we can bless again
> The drumming of an army,
> The steady, soaking rain
> Core of my heart my country!
> Land of the Rainbow Gold
> For flood and fire and famine,
> She pays us back threefold
> Over the thirsty paddocks
> Watch, after many days,
> The filmy veil of greenness
> That thickens as we gaze
> An opal-hearted country,
> A wilful, lavish land
> All you, who have not loved her,
> You will not understand
> Though earth holds many splendours,
> Wherever I may die,
> I know to what brown country
> My homing thought will fly.
>
> *My Country by Dorothea Mackellar*

LEARN A LITTLE ITALIAN

FAMILY

Padre	father
Madre	mother
Fratello	brother
Sorella	sister
Nonno	grandfather
Nonna	grandmother
Bisnonno	great-grandfather
Bisnonna	great-grandmother
Marito	husband
Moglia	wife
Figlia	daughter
Figlio	son
Figli	children
Zio	uncle
Zia	auntie
Cugino	male cousin
Cugina	female cousin
Cuginetti	little cousins
Cognata	sister-in-law
Cognato	brother-in-law
Famiglia	family
Padrino	godfather
Madrina	godmother
Compare	best man
Commare	matron of honour
Amici	friends
Amico	male friend
Amica	female friend
Uomo	male
Bambini	children
Nipoti	nieces/nephews/grandchildren

EATING/ MEALTIMES

Mangiare	eat
Festa	feast
Voglio	I want
Pranzo	lunch
Cena	dinner
Colazione	breakfast
Buone appetito	good appetite
Grazie	thank you
Prego	you're welcome
Buonissimo	very good
Vino	wine
Aqua	water

GREETINGS

Buongiorno	good morning
Salve	hi
Ciao	hello
Arrivedeci	see you later
Buona note	good night

FOOD AND COOKING

Ordori	herbs
Pane	bread
Farina	flour
Verdura	green vegetables
Aqua	water
Forno	oven
Fuoco	fire
Cucina	cooking

MISCELLANEOUS

Sole	sun
Vento	wind
Vita	life
Mondo	world
Cuore	heart
Sognare	dream
Credere	believe
Rispetto	respect
Leale	loyal
Feducia	trust
Onore	honour
Appassionato	passionate
Corraggio	courage
Accetare	accept
Radici	roots
Caminare	walk
Donna	woman
Feminine	female
Amore	love
Gioa	joy
Tesoro	treasure
Bella	nice
Dolce	sweet
Voi	do you
Baci	kiss

TIMES OF THE DAY

Giornata	today
Pommeriggio	afternoon
Notte/sera	night
Giorno	day

ITALIAN SAYINGS

Meglio un giorno da un leone che cento da pecora.
Better one day a lion than a hundred years a sheep.

Chi va piano va sano e lontano.
He who goes slow and steady goes a long way.

I mei radici.
My roots.

La Tavola.
The table.

Contentati con puoco che asai avrai.
Be happy with little and you will have a lot.

Guai.
Trouble/watch out.

Silenzio e d'oro.
Silence is golden.

Il dolce far niente.
The sweetness of doing nothing.

Chi va a letto senza cena tutta la notte si dimena.
He who goes to bed without eating will regret it throughout the night.

Mangiare per vivere e non vivere per mangiare.
Eat to live and not live to eat.

A tavola non si invecchia.
At the table with good friends and family you do not become old.

La cucina piccola fal la casa grande.
A small kitchen makes the house big.

Pan di sudore, miglior sapore.
Bread that comes out of sweat, tastes better.

Non si vive di solo pane.
One does not live by bread alone.

Chi mangia sulo s'affoga.
He who eats alone suffocates.

O mangi questa minestra o salti dalla finestra.
You eat this soup or you jump out the window.

Piatto ricco, mi ci ficco.
Rich plate, I dive in it.

Gallina vecchia fa buon brodo.
Old chicken makes good broth.

L'ospite è come il pesce: dopo tre giorni puzza.
The guest is like fish: he smells after three days.

Tutto fa brodo.
Everything makes broth.

Buon vino fa sangue.
Good wine makes good blood.

Una mela al giorno toglie il medico di torno.
An apple a day keeps the doctor away.

Chi dorme non prende pesci.
He who sleeps does not catch fish.

Master of Cucina Povera
Authentic Sicilian Cooking

Disclaimer:
The material in this publication is of general nature only, and does not represent professional advice. It is not intended to provide specific guidance for particular circumstances and it should not be relied on as the basis of any decision to take action or not to take action on matters which it covers. Readers should obtain professional advice where appropriate, before making any such decision. the author and publisher disclaim all responsibility and liability to any person, arising directly or indirectly from any person taking or not taking action based on the information in this publication.

Carmela's Cucina Povera:
A Journey of Self-Discovery and Healing through Sicilian Cooking
First published in Australia in 2015 by Carmela D'Amore.

© Carmela D'Amore 2015:
The moral right of the author has been asserted.

All rights reserved. Without limiting the rights under copyright restricted above, no part of this publication may be produced, stored in a retrieval system, or transmitted in any form or by any means (electronic, mechanical, photocopying, recording or otherwise), without the prior written permission of the publisher.

National Library of Australian Catalouge -in- Publication entry

Author:	Carmela (Amato) D'Amore
Editor:	Cavalletti Communications - Daniela Cavalletti and Ella Legg
Title:	Carmela's Cucina Povera: A Journey of Self-Discovery and Healing through Sicilian Cooking
ISBN:	978-0-9942329-7-7
Artwork & Design:	Dave McIntosh - Email: david@hmcreative.com.au
Food Stylist:	Lisa Hart
Photography:	Dave McIntosh - Mobile: 0408 39 44 50
Print:	Printed in Australia by Nicholas and Vivienne Kane - Excite Print
Authors Note:	I would like to extremely thank Nick Sutherland from State of Mind Therapy and Polly (his dog) for all of the guidance and support to get me through to the next stage in my life.

Giuseppe (Pepe) Maiorana.
-Bisnonno